everyday Bliss
for busy women

Energy Balancing Secrets for
Complete Health & Vitality

MARYAM WEBSTER, M.ED.

New Harbinger Publications, Inc.

Publisher's Note

This publication is designed to provide accurate and authoritative information in regard to the subject matter covered. It is sold with the understanding that the publisher is not engaged in rendering psychological, financial, legal, or other professional services. If expert assistance or counseling is needed, the services of a competent professional should be sought.

Distributed in Canada by Raincoast Books

Copyright © 2008 by Maryam Webster
New Harbinger Publications, Inc.
5674 Shattuck Avenue
Oakland, CA 94609
www.newharbinger.com

Cover and text design by Amy Shoup; Graphics by Matthew Dixon;
Author photo by Jason Frankenfield; Acquired by Jess O'Brien; Edited by Amy Johnson

Library of Congress Cataloging-in-Publication Data

Webster, Maryam.
  Everyday bliss for busy women : energy balancing secrets for complete health and vitality
/ Maryam Webster.
     p. cm.
  Includes bibliographical references.
  ISBN-13: 978-1-57224-567-9 (pbk. : alk. paper)
  ISBN-10: 1-57224-567-0 (pbk. : alk. paper) 1. Women--Health and hygiene. 2. Vitality.
3. Women--Mental health. 4. Happiness. I. Title.
  RA778.W227 2008
  613'.04244--dc22
                              2008003625

10   09   08

10   9   8   7   6   5   4   3   2   1

First printing

This book is dedicated to my mother, Winona Doris Ratliff Russell. Mom had tremendous faith in me and was an outspoken advocate for bliss in my life, even when struggles with pain and physical disability clouded my path. This book is also dedicated to devoted mothers worldwide, whose selfless love and advocacy enable children who might never have done so otherwise to walk, talk, dance, and sing. Moms, consider this book a thank-you present for a job well done.

Contents

Acknowledgments

$\mathcal{F}$irst, I would like to thank Joseph Campbell, that dear mythologist who enjoined us all to "follow your bliss," and gave me the idea to write this book. Thanks also to my spiritual mentor, the metís shaman Corliss "d" deLarm Jr. who showed me the path of bliss in my own life.

This book would not have been possible without the many coaching clients who helped me refine the Everyday Bliss Process through its diligent application in their own lives. Though I have changed names to protect identities, the examples in this book are taken from the lives of real women with jobs, problems, and issues just like yours. My thanks go to them and also to the "Women of Bliss" who graciously gave of their time to be interviewed. Though I was only able to include a fraction of these interviews in the book, every single one aided my research and I am grateful to each interviewee. You can hear and read many of these interviews at the book's website: www.everydaybliss.org.

I also wish to acknowledge the contributions of John Thie, Donna Eden, David Feinstein, Gary Craig, Larry Nims, and Tapas Fleming, who developed many of the tools you will find in this book. I am particularly grateful to ZPoint Process creator Grant Connolly for his great cooperation and collegial sharing in writing the ZPoint chapter.

Thanks also go to my teachers and primary influences in the field of Neurolinguistic Programming: Tim Halbom, Robert Dilts, Suzi Smith, and the members of the NLP Café. The field is rich with contributions from different sources, many of which have informed my work—thank you all for what you do.

Personal thanks goes to my husband, Jason, and to the Friday Morning WWBD Mastermind group, both of which endured paragraph-by-paragraph dissections with grace and good humor, always coming up with good input.

Thanks also to my editors at New Harbinger. You've been gracious, accommodating, and unfailingly kind throughout this process. I couldn't have done it without you.

Finally I would like to acknowledge the Everyday Bliss R&D Team, who tested the concepts at www.everydaybliss.org and gave generously of their feedback. It's been a pleasure to create a book with you that will truly make a difference in people's lives.

—*Maryam Webster*
San Francisco, California
August 2007

Foreword

All those years ago when I wrote *The Woman's Comfort Book*, I didn't know I was going to be lucky enough to be a small part of a luminous, glorious movement devoted to mindfulness, passion, and sanity that was just getting its start. What began as a few voices saying, "Um, I think this self-care stuff might be important, I think the way modern life is going might not be all good" has become a tidal wave of books, TV programs, radio shows, seminars, and one-on-one conversations exploring the myriad ways we can create a life that is sustainable, founded on simplicity, and guided by something more compelling and alive than how much money we earn or how young we look. We're constantly discovering new ways to live the truth that self-care, self-nurturing and work/life flow are not luxuries but instead, they're part of the solution to our survival as a species. It's about a whole lot more than chocolate and hot baths.

Maryam Webster knows this and that's why her book is important —from her well-researched information on energy cultivation to her practical pointers on getting your mind around how you choose to spend your time, these pages offer more of what we need to keep evolving, to keep learning new thrive. Because it's clear: the world is not slowing down. Nobody "out there" is going to be pushing the universal pause button anytime soon. It's up to each of us to say "Enough already," whether that enough already is not buying into the story that your kids will fall behind if you don't have them scheduled every micro second, or discovering that buying more stuff doesn't actually fill the void in your heart, or learning that taking time to catch up with yourself does not cause anyone, including yourself, to die.

You know you can't live in this postmodern world without it taking a ginormous physical, emotional, and spiritual toll on you, and you know that if you don't get really, really smart and creative about how you deal with the onslaught of busyness, information, and change that comes at you almost every moment, you'll die, if not physically, then certainly spiritually and emotionally. Maryam offers easy and effective help in *Everyday Bliss for Busy Women*, so why not take a long, sweet breath and promise yourself you'll try at least one idea from this treasure trove today? Why not resist the urge to believe that simply owning the book is enough, and that it will help you from its spot on the shelf? We are what we practice. We become what we do. I vote for becoming more sane, more alive, and more able to express and share your unique energy with the world by doing more than buying or even reading this book: Put it to use. Let it become dog-eared, tea stained, and chocolate smeared (I didn't say chocolate was passe) as it helps you create a life rich in awareness, positive energy, and gratitude for all that you are. You are deserving.

—Jennifer Louden
Bainbridge Island, Washington 2008

Everyday Bliss for Busy Women

This book is for every woman out there who is overcommitted, underenergized, and chronically behind schedule. This book is for every woman whose physical body, emotional life, or relationships are suffering as a result of running close to empty There is help in these pages for every woman who comes in from shopping, dropping off kids, appointments, or a day at the office feeling half-dead but with still more work to tackle before she gets any time for herself—assuming she ever *does* get any time to herself. There are processes, reminders, and quick feel-good help in this book for every woman who doesn't even remember what bliss is, let alone what bliss actually feels like. I wrote this book for every woman who passionately longs to regain the sense of ease, relaxation, joy, clarity, and mental and physical space in life known as everyday bliss.

In my energy coaching practice, the women business and community leaders I work with are tremendously overstressed and overcommitted. Whether they have families or are living the single life, they often describe themselves as feeling frustrated and numb after a hard day's work. Most of the time, a good night's sleep is not enough to recharge their batteries. From these conditions arise anger and further frustration, which lead to stress-related health problems and relationship difficulties. Many feel unable to control the emotions, content, and context of their days. But it doesn't have to be this way.

You *can* work your way out of overstress and overcommitment on your own and leverage more time, peace, and delight in your life. You *can* reteach yourself to literally live in everyday bliss. And by everyday bliss, I don't mean staying in a meditative state every second of the day, but reorienting your life away from stress, overcommitment, and endless "have to's" toward spaciousness, relaxation, and calm. By using the cutting-edge techniques you'll learn in this book, you can make small mental shifts and reduce your stress permanently. You'll learn, too, how to luxuriate your way into exquisite self-care and equanimity in any situation so that bliss becomes a natural state, every day.

This isn't an empty promise. I was in severe, toxic stress for nearly a decade and, though it took focus, moved past it into bliss. I've also spent the last twenty-five years helping my psychotherapy and coaching clients find their own bliss. With our busy lives, if we can find not only our bliss but re-create it every day, you can too.

WHY I WROTE THIS BOOK

In 1988 I was hit by a drunk driver. My back was broken, and I ended up bedridden for three years, partially paralyzed from the waist down. It took me a further six years to recover my mobility. My marriage to a brilliant but destructive alcoholic fell apart, and I was left lying in bed with few resources and next to no hope of bettering my situation. The physical agony alone was excruciating, but, cheered on by a mother who never lost faith in me, I began looking for alternatives to the mind-numbing pain drugs and antidepressants, alternatives that might actually help me regain my life.

Never underestimate the power of a determined woman: in the face of doctors telling me I might never walk again, I went from a walker to two crutches, to two canes, to one cane, and slowly, very slowly, over nearly a decade, to walking unaided. Today, nearly twenty years later, though not without the occasional hitch, I am walking, dancing, and hiking again—largely due to the presence of energy therapies.

The first of these, Emotional Freedom Technique (EFT), worked like a miracle. I was floored by how quickly it took away not only the pain, but also other unwanted symptoms, like the nightmarish memory of the accident that played over and over. Touch For Health, Educational Kinesiology, and Neurolinguistic Programming (NLP) further healed me, and the newer therapies of Tapas Acupressure Technique (TAT) and ZPoint Process proved to be very effective personal-transformation techniques. What I loved even more was that the newer methods were easy to learn. Virtually anyone—even children—can learn to use these techniques to help themselves out of everyday physical and emotional difficulty.

During my years of recovery, I retrained as a personal performance coach. Incorporating the best of human achievement techniques with energy therapies, I codified a new profession: energy coaching. I began teaching my Certified Energy Coach Program in 2003; today it is offered through the Energy Coach Institute (www.energycoachinstitute.com). In these programs I teach health and wellness professionals to bust through blockages—blockages that might once have taken months or years of work—in only minutes or hours, with the very energy therapies you'll learn in this book.

I invite you to use these tools not only to help yourself, but also to help your entire family reduce stress and be happy. Teach these methods to your family and friends. They are easy to learn and use and can both promote overall wellness and de-stress you in mere minutes. As you become comfortable with these bliss-inducers, they can also be used to safely release decades-old blockages to create a relaxed and success-oriented lifestyle.

I wrote this book to share these amazing but little-known wellness tools with others in need. I wrote this book to bring the Everyday Bliss Process to women like myself, who face insurmountable odds and need to find a better way, a way that is simple, side-effect free, fast-acting, and—most importantly—works to induce bliss, every single time.

I wrote this book for *you*.

THE UNIQUE DIFFERENCE OF THE EVERYDAY BLISS PROCESS

While many books have been written on how to live a more relaxed life, this book, unlike the rest, contains a unique set of "energy wellness" tools that have until now only been known to some hundreds of therapy clients and lay practitioners. These are the methods that took away my pain and finally got me walking again. Energy therapies can be used not only to address pain and bodily dysfunction, but also to eliminate the limiting beliefs and crippling emotions that keep us from reaching true success in our lives. Hundreds of people use energy therapies every second of the day with wonderful results on a whole range of issues.

How the Energy of Negativity Works in the Human Body

When an upsetting event occurs, the body begins to produce adrenaline, cortisol, and other damaging, stress-related chemicals. These stress hormones act as the building blocks of a neurochemical "lock" that bolts the feeling of the upsetting event, memory, or situation deeply into the body's tissues. Without even knowing it, a new knot of muscular tension appears in the stomach, neck, shoulders, or back. Such knots always have a mental/emotional component and also exist in the mind as tension and anxiety. In conducting our everyday affairs, we tend to steer away from these knots without even realizing it. Over time these knots will harden into general tendencies that keep us from

5

experiencing true peace and relaxation. Unchecked, stress can build in the body for years.

The Different Kinds of Energy Therapies

There are two main types of energy therapy methods: meridian-based and intentional. *Meridian-based* methods, which include Tapas Acupressure Technique and Emotional Freedom Technique, tap into the ancient science of acupuncture. Your body naturally produces its own energy in the form of a weak electromagnetic current. From this, a subtle energy field, often called the *aura*, extends to create an envelope around your body. This energy also courses through specific channels in your body, known in acupuncture as *meridians*. The energy in these meridians can be accessed and modified through power points on the surface of your skin. Many ancient cultures worldwide have used these powerful energy centers to heal and de-stress.

Acupuncturists insert needles into power points on these meridians in order to cure diseases and alter an individual's entire wellness pattern. Similarly, by holding or gently tapping different sequences of meridian points with our fingertips, we can both reduce—or even eliminate—stress and generate emotional and physical well-being.

Intentional energy therapy methods, which include Be Set Free Fast (BSFF), ZPoint Process, and Neurolinguistic Programming, feature advanced relaxation techniques and emotion-management practices that use only the power of intention and the electromagnetic current produced in the brain to effect change. With these methods there is no tapping or holding of points. Instead, you read a simple set of instructions and choose a cue word, which you then employ, using a series of mental steps to change whatever issue you've chosen to work on.

In this book you'll learn both meridian-based and intentional energy therapies in several different formats. Having this rich toolset at hand will help you choose which method or methods you personally find most comfortable to use on a daily basis. These methods are drug-free and easy to practice, and they require no gizmos—just your mind, a willing heart, and, in some cases, your hands.

While energy therapies can at times produce miracles and are, as far as is presently known, side-effect free, they should not be used as a replacement for appropriate health care from qualified medical or psychotherapy professionals. Use good judgment in applying energy therapies in your own life; if you're experiencing severe symptoms, get professional help.

WE'RE ALL HEALING FROM SOMETHING

If you're reading this book, chances are you, too, are trying to recover from the destructive nature of modern life. Cardinal symptoms of this kind of lifestyle include feeling as though you never have enough time or privacy, feeling that you have too many worries, feeling that you haven't accomplished all you should have, and feeling behind the curve and as if you'll never quite catch up or that you've only just caught up but will be behind before morning. There may be a subtle nagging in the corner of your mind, just out of view sometimes, that you're not good enough, not fast enough, and that it will never, ever all be "done."

If you can't remember the last time you truly felt relaxed, you could be putting your health at risk. Depression is often a side-effect of a high-stress lifestyle (Kiecolt-Glaser, Glaser, and McGuire 2002). Further, the University of Illinois at Chicago's heart-health database cites a 2.5 times greater risk for heart attack in stressed people with active depression (2004). If this is you, take heart: the resources in this book can help you to detoxify the difficult areas of your life, reduce stress, and dramatically improve your health.

WHERE'S MY BLISS?

Wondering if you really need to learn the methods this book has to offer you? Take the following true-or-false quiz. Give yourself one point for each "false" answer:

1. I have enough time in my life to get everything necessary done. I don't stress about time and feel I have enough space and downtime in my daily schedule.

2. I can name three things that must be present in order for me to have a blissful, relaxing experience.

3. I am consistently able to handle unexpected frustrations easily and without undue stress.

4. Within the last three months I took a break from the routine of my life (either at home or away) that was long enough for me to feel relaxed and rejuvenated.

5. I almost never get angry and am known for my sense of calm.

Now total up your score. How did you do? If you scored more than two points, stress is a serious problem for you and could be causing changes in your metabolism (stress hormones cause us to pack on fat, too), heart health (which worsens in situations where you are frustrated and angry), and mental function (depression and other mental dysfunctions have their roots in chronic stress; Kiecolt-Glaser, Glaser, and McGuire 2002).

THE EVERYDAY BLISS PROCESS

In this book, you'll learn the Everyday Bliss Process in much the same way my coaching clients learn it. Like them you'll use the Everyday Bliss Process to coach yourself back to a peaceful life. The process itself consists of seven simple phases, outlined below.

Though this book is written in an organic, free-flowing style, the beginning of each chapter is highlighted with the particular phase of the Bliss Process the chapter covers.

Phase 1: Creating Blissful Space

Phase 1 consists of setting aside the space for bliss to manifest in your life. That means making space for bliss, both mentally and physically. In this phase, if you haven't already done so, you'll create a personal altar or meditation space. If you already have one, rededicate that area to cultivation of your everyday bliss.

Phase 2: Personal Assessment

In this phase, you'll decide what bliss means to you and make a Bliss List. What brings bliss into your life? What really turns you on and feels delicious? You'll use this list to restore bliss to your daily living.

Phase 3: Getting Real

Presumably you're reading this because you feel your life could either be better or more peaceful, calm, and relaxed. In phase 3 you'll examine what in your life is out of whack or overwhelming. You'll look at the places where life isn't so beautiful, digging as far back into the past as possible. This may be a bit unpleasant, but it's necessary because, using the tools in this book, you're going to change all of the negative elements—you're going to embrace the life you've always wanted! From this fearless self-examination you'll make a Shadow List of those things that block you from everyday bliss.

Phase 4: Your Life Mission

To truly live in bliss, you need to understand your unique mission in life. What will make you truly, deeply happy to focus your life on? What must you accomplish in this life before you die? When you focus your life through the lens of a passionate mission, stress recedes, and fulfillment becomes automatic. In this phase, you'll identify and refine your life mission.

Phase 5: Your Treasure Map to Bliss

In phase 5, you'll examine what you really want in your daily life—the state you desire to live in every day. By this I don't mean just a better car or new house, but how you want to feel on the inside, day in and day out, how your daily life can fulfill and support you and your life mission. In this phase you'll focus on what your internal state feels like, the kind of people you want in your life and how you want them to treat you, and how your outer environment can change your inner state.

Phase 6: Resolve Your Bliss Blockers and Employ the Bliss Keys

Next, in phase 6, you'll use the transformation tools found in this book to take charge of your life and eliminate the Bliss Blockers of your Shadow List. Simultaneously, you'll start doing a simple "energy hygiene" routine in the morning and evening and learn to drop into a blissful state of mind whenever you like, using the Bliss Keys. Just by themselves, these keys will help funnel comfort and joy into your life.

Phase 7: Test, Amend, Repeat

It's important to make sure that the corrections you're implementing via energy therapies are working—in phase 7, the final phase, you'll test your results rigorously. When you finish clearing away an upsetting incident, make sure you reimagine the situation or blockage you were working on. Hear the words that upset you, see the scene, feel the feelings. If any negativity whatsoever still remains, continue to apply the clearing methods until your tests show the situation is completely clear. Test also a week or so down the line on the first few things you clear, just to prove to yourself that what you're doing is working.

WHAT YOU WILL LEARN IN THIS BOOK

The Everyday Bliss Process that you'll begin in chapter 1 will take you from feeling overwhelmed to enjoying blissful relaxation and personal peace in your everyday life. From the start of chapter 1, you'll begin to implement simple shifts in consciousness and personal action. The foundation of this process lies in the Bliss Keys. By themselves, these keys will rocket you past most of your tension and into a more relaxed and expansive lifestyle. Using only the energy in your own body, triggered by situations that naturally occur in your day (waking, lunchtime, unwanted feelings, problematic issues, homecoming, and bedtime), the Everyday Bliss Process will help you sweeten your everyday existence from morning to night. And to wrap it all up, the Everyday Bliss Process will help you create a plan for an entire *year* of bliss, with things to do every month and every day to get more bliss into your life.

Throughout the book, you'll meet phenomenal women from all walks of life, women just like you and me, who are exemplars of bliss; each has a valuable lesson to share. You'll also have the freedom to choose from both quick-start "instant relaxers" that only take a few minutes and comprehensive methods that can help you clear the more complicated issues that block your joy in life. (For a quick start right now, jump to chapter 4 and start getting your sense of inner peace back on track.)

Everyday Bliss energy exercises are easy, doable, and can be practiced in minutes, even invisibly and in front of others. I know: I've used them on planes, in class, and while presenting in front of both large audiences and intimate board meetings. I've used these tools to take myself from the paralysis of a broken back into complete mobility and personal freedom on all levels. And if I can do it, so can you.

Are you ready? Great! Let's begin your journey to bliss.

CHAPTER 1

Redefining "Selfish" and
Reclaiming Extra Time

$\mathcal{I}$t may not come tomorrow, but if you're a working woman (and this most definitely includes stay-at-home moms), chances are your wake-up call will come sooner rather than later—the siren signal that all is not well in your world, that things are, in fact, very much out of balance, that your cup is close to being drained dry. And when you're at this point, everyday bliss may seem far from possible. But it is achievable, and this book will help you bring it back into your life.

**This chapter relates to phases 1–3 of the
Everyday Bliss Process, outlined on pages 9 and 10.**

For coaching-world entrepreneur Andrea Lee, the call back to everyday bliss came in the form of heart palpitations, insomnia, tremendous surges of anger, and so strong a feeling of being overwhelmed that she feared she was about to die. In 2002, Andrea was general manager of CoachVille, then the world's largest personal and business coaching organization. When its charismatic founder Thomas Leonard died of a sudden heart attack, CoachVille was thrown into turmoil; its forty thousand member coaches all looked to Andrea to make sense of things. In trying to care for others, Andrea, as so many of us do, drained herself dangerously dry. "A spontaneous acupuncture appointment literally saved my life," she says. "My body was really leaving me—I thought I was going to die. And it was only then that I paid attention."

Heeding her body's frantic distress calls, Andrea dropped back and found her bliss again—but not without some effort. "It was worth it though," she says with a soft smile. "I'd have died if I'd kept up that pace." To rebalance, she now regularly engages in a meditative practice of Feldenkrais and takes time for herself, which she uses to hang out with her two dogs and husband, linger in bubble baths, listen to "loud music, *really* loud music!" and just think.

She smiles more now and has deliciously slow but rich thoughts that bring abundance without struggle to her Andrea J. Lee Group of Companies (www.andreajlee.com). Her marital relationship, once fractured, has healed and become sweet again. Palpitations and stomach sourness are things of the past. Slowing down, she says, was one of the keys to her bliss.

DEDICATE YOURSELF TO A LIFE OF EVERYDAY BLISS

Odds are that you, like Andrea, live at least part of your life at warp speed. Who doesn't nowadays? Take five minutes right now to sit down, become quiet (no TV, radio, iPod, or other distractions), and dedicate yourself to your own well-being.

First, find a mirror large enough to see your whole face in. Sit in a quiet place and silently affirm yourself to be in a separate time and space from the rest of the world. If you wish, light candles or incense. Next, look into your eyes in the mirror and affirm to yourself:

> *I am worth putting first in my life. I am enough, just as I am. Nothing requires me to go at light speed. What is meant for me can never be lost and will always be there. There is no need to rush; I can take as much time as needed for what is important. I dedicate myself to exquisite self-care and the cultivation of everyday bliss in my life. I am worth this.*

CREATING A BLISSFUL SPACE

If you don't already have one, please craft yourself a personal altar. This isn't a religious altar but a place—at home or the office—that you can go to for personal sustenance throughout your day. Situate your altar in a small corner of your bedroom, home office, or some other room that you can shut the world out of; keep this space continually devoted to your Everyday Bliss work. For the altar itself, you can use anything from a corner of a bookcase to a small table you keep just for that purpose. Dress it up with whatever items remind you of peace, relaxation, and being in harmony with your universe.

Also, keep a small icon that symbolizes your bliss practice at work. Choose something that will blend in with your desk items—this could be a stone, small figurine, candle, or other small object. This object is a secret signal to you throughout your work week that will remind you to use the Everyday Bliss Process.

As you go deeper into the Everyday Bliss Process, make your altar truly portable by creating your "ideal" personal development space in your mind. Daydream: If you could have your altar anywhere in the world, in space, time, and place, where would it be? What would you want in this inner altar space? What would it look like, feel like, and smell like? How would you feel when you are here? In many meditation traditions, this is called "building the inner temple." This inner sanctuary is a powerful place you can go to for renewal.

As Without, So Within

My client Cheryl, the headmistress of a county school system in a large city in southern England, longed for the country lanes of her youth. Cheryl remembered a neighbor's folly, a miniature Greek temple similar to a gazebo that she played in as a child, as a place she always felt at peace. In her teens it became a refuge for her whenever stress threatened. This folly was demolished long ago, but it lives on now in her mind, as her inner altar.

When we first began working on this inner altar, Cheryl laughed and said, "Those old cushions I brought here twenty years ago are pretty moldy!" She changed those moldy cushions right then for brand-new, silk-covered cushions and added bolsters and scarf-draped divans. She even added bowls of fresh fruit and flowers and imagined a small waterfall into being.

As we finished the session, Cheryl sighed deeply and said, with tears gathering in her eyes, "I didn't know how very much I missed this place. I didn't realize how long it had been since I felt so deeply at peace." Cheryl now goes to her inner altar multiple times a day, briefly to refresh for a moment, and for more extended periods to meditate and do her bliss work.

You, like Cheryl, may already have a place deeply anchored inside you where you feel comfortable, safe, and calm. These remembered places often resonate deeply with us. If you don't remember such a place, you can, of course, invent one from scratch.

RECLAIMING AND REDEFINING YOUR BLISS

If you're not experiencing bliss today, here's how you can retool your thinking to do so. Turn off all of the electronic "assistants" that you have—the phone, the television, the computer, your cell phone. Now, take a few moments before you dive into the rest of this book to simply redefine bliss for yourself.

First, what *is* bliss, anyway? It could be anything from relaxing into a bubble bath or a massage and feeling all your muscles release to the delicious taste of artisan chocolates, from the joy you feel at watching your child play to the warm snuggling of your pet. Bliss might be watching a beautiful sunset, getting home from work early, or having the report you need to turn in done a day before it's due. It can be anything you want.

To regain the bliss in your life, you'll first need to know both what bliss means to *you*, and what keeps you from experiencing bliss every day. To do this you'll create two lists. (You'll use these lists in exercises throughout the book; I'll explain more about this in the next section.) I suggest that you also journal about everything you do that's related to regaining your bliss. This will give you a record of successes that you can refer back to on days when things don't seem quite so blissful. In the front of your Bliss Journal, put the following two lists.

Your Bliss List

Write down on your Bliss List at least ten things that bring you true joy. Focus on small things that make you feel delicious, wonderful, and nurtured. Starting small is essential. Defining bliss as big package—a whole day at the spa for instance—will make it difficult to achieve on a daily basis. What is a small thing that gives you deep joy? This could be something as simple as watching a flower open, eating a perfectly ripe peach, savoring the feeling of your tired feet sliding into warm bath water, or seeing happiness spread across the face of your child, partner, or pet as you come through the door.

Make sure that you include on your Bliss List at least three things that you can implement yourself, like bubble baths or other self-care treats. Do one of these things for yourself today. Choose another tomorrow. If you want to be especially generous and kind to yourself, choose more than one. Consult your Bliss List whenever you want to treat yourself and relax.

Your Shadow List

Address in your Shadow List anything that bothers you or makes you feel bad about yourself. These items could include upsetting incidents from your past, traits in yourself that you don't like, and any embarrassing or demoralizing memories you'd rather not have. You'll work on the items on this Shadow List with the energy therapies you'll learn in this book. You'll be using these two lists in later chapters, so keep them handy.

THE TYRANNY OF TIME

There are three things you must know to free yourself from the tyranny of time:

- Multitasking is impossible.

- We cannot "do it all."

- Superwoman does not exist except in fiction.

Trying to accomplish too much in too little time can lead to illness, frustration, and relationship problems. Let's all just stop driving ourselves too hard and instead embrace a saner, more rational way to live.

Start by meditating deeply on two of the fundamental precepts of everyday bliss:

- Nothing is truly required of you.

- You are the primary source of your own stress.

Serious survival duties aside, most of what we feel we "gotta/hafta" do is self-generated. It's not uncommon for panic in others to bring out a similar response in us. Your child feels stressed; you feel stressed. Your upset boss comes thundering into your office; you become upset. This automatic reaction catapults you headlong into the body's adrenalinized fight-or-flight response. But this reaction doesn't have to be automatic—the more you become aware of your reaction, the more it becomes a choice. And you can choose not to participate.

The idea that nothing is required of you is radical but true. Survival is the one exception, the one defining biological imperative that we have. Leaving a life-threatening situation is a survival duty required of you: you must do it to preserve the health of the body. Beyond this, however, actions become choices, though we may not always think they are. For example, constantly attending to others' emergencies *isn't* required of us, yet it is a behavioral pattern that many of us were taught in some form or another. Your choice to respond to others' stress and confusion is fundamentally that—a choice. The saying is true: "Lack of planning on your part does not constitute an emergency on my part." Constantly responding to emergencies not of your own making takes a lot of time out of your day, week, month, and year.

Time reclamation can be done, but it requires some planning. If you're like most women today, you're running at top speed for at least some portion of your day or week. (If you're wondering about this, check your quiz results from the introduction.) To reclaim some time for yourself—even if you have a busy life and just can't think of how you're going to shoehorn another single second out of it—the first thing you have to do is slow down.

"What?!" I can hear you saying. "Impossible! I have a board meeting tomorrow and a PTA meeting tonight. My sister's coming to visit in the morning, and I'm way behind on the Stevens contract. And I still have to pick Jimmy up from band and Ellie up from soccer and take them to piano and play practice."

Right. Exactly. I get your drift. Now get mine: You can do this. Really. I have faith in you, and as my mom would tell you, anything I have faith in had better just give up. I've put a powerful load of belief (a form of energy we'll be getting to in the next chapter) into you. Plus, I happen to know that this stuff works, even for kindergarteners. You can do this. Really, you can!

So, just to start, think about three ways you can slow down. Implement one of these three this week, a second next week, and the third the week after that. Doing one a week will make it simple and give your system time to adjust to slowing down. Speaking of slowing down, could you use some extra time? Who couldn't. Let's generate some now.

How Time Gets Away from Us

"How did my entire day get away from me with only three emails to show for it? How on earth could this have happened?!" This came through my instant messenger window from an otherwise very successful client, who is a well-known museum patron and art-world maven. That particular day, in addition to running her successful chain of galleries, Jennifer found herself cleaning gutters, doing dishes, handwashing delicate laundry, and sorting her holiday wrapping paper—in June. These were all projects she could have easily put off for days, weeks, or even months. Because of these "important projects" she was going crazy trying to find even five minutes for herself, much less finish writing the materials for her next docent training course.

When we looked at why Jennifer was so overbooked, we found one big problem and one minor one. First, instead of working in a quiet place, Jennifer regularly worked in the living room with the television switched on. When I put it to her that in a corporate job she would never even think of watching television during a work day, she agreed and selected two half-hour informational programs from her list to watch as coffee-break type treats.

Second, Jennifer spent a lot of time searching for advertising graphics when an assistant could have done it just as well. She told herself that it was important for her to do this and all of her other tasks, that no one else could do them like she could. Sometimes this is true—often it isn't. Doing tasks that don't require your personal attention eats up time you could be using for those important tasks that *do* require your personal attention.

Time Reclamation Project

Make a list of the things you do that fritter away time needlessly. Include things that you do out of season, like Jennifer's holiday paper sorting, and things that are addictive, time-sucking habits, such as endless crafts projects, online game playing, television watching, or Web surfing.

Now, identify the "must-do's" on this list—if indeed there are any. Often you'll find there aren't. However, if there are "must-do's," choose your top three to work on in the morning and top three to work on in the afternoon. Or simply shortlist four or five to work on all day. If an opportunity to do something comes up ("Oprah's on in ten minutes!" "There's a sale at the grocery store!" "Better take care of those dishes before they multiply!"), compare this to your list for the day. Isn't on the list? Then you're not doing it. Start a second list of things to do when your work is done, and put all the nonwork items on it. If you feel like it, after the close of business, handle some of these items. Alternatively, outsource them.

If you're like Jennifer, you can job out much of your busywork at home and on the job. For home, hire a maid service, hire a high school kid to mow the yard, outsource the laundry, or draft your kids to help (and don't accept excuses). Insofar as possible, find someone to help you do time-consuming tasks that are paid at below your salary or hourly range. If your budget is tight, try sharing tasks on a rotating basis with neighbors, friends, or others in similar situations—for example, you help me with the tough gardening job today, and I'll babysit your kids next Tuesday. At work, you can similarly coordinate with coworkers to round-robin less attractive busywork tasks.

When you job out things that don't provide much return on a time investment, you send a message to the universe that says: "I value myself enough to create more time in my life for me." As you create more time by not involving yourself in the busywork of your life, you will not only have the time to finally get your work done, you'll also have more time for yourself.

TIME EXPANSION EXPERIMENT

1. This week, monitor all of the things you feel you "gotta/
   hafta" do. Write them down and look at them at the end
   of the week. Did you really have to do all those things
   the second you felt your stress rising? Could you have
   planned better, delegated or deferred some of these items,
   or deleted some of them entirely from your list? Take
   another sheet of paper and write down:

   Do | Defer | Delegate | Delete

   This activity will help you really clear the decks. Get
   out your trusty list-making materials. "Do" items are tasks
   to be done today or tomorrow. "Defer" items are those
   tasks to be done later this week or next week. "Delegate"
   items are those you can get someone else to do. "Delete"
   items are those you're going to permanently or at least
   semi-permanently drop from your life—anything you
   know you won't have time to get to in the next three to
   six months. Sort all of your "gotta/hafta's" into these four
   headings. If you find you've been piling everything under
   "Do," get tough with yourself, and re-sort. Add the "gotta/
   hafta's" that hang on the longest to your Shadows List.

2. Delegate with grace. You can delegate much of your life
   nowadays and regain huge amounts of money, time, and
   sanity doing so. If you can take your delegation tasks
   to overseas virtual assistants, such as those that can be

found at Guru.com or Elance.com (who can plan everything from buying tickets to updating your website; from conducting research to making reservations for dinner), help can only cost a few dollars an hour. If you can get something done for less than half your hourly wage, you may want to consider it. Even if it may pinch your budget a bit to start, getting a housekeeper in to handle big cleaning chores can go a long way to restoring your sanity. And you'll have that time back for yourself. Make sure your budget can truly take the expenditure however, before allocating funds for such a service.

So, what are you delegating this week? How much time have you recouped? And, more importantly, what are you doing with it?

The Importance of Writing and Reading

As I mentioned earlier, it's important keep a Bliss Journal to note your problems, what you're working on, and—most importantly— what gives you bliss. This has proven to be an excellent tool to help women both recapture their bliss and remember what's important in their lives. You don't have to be a good writer and you can be as messy as you want—the Bliss Journal is only for you.

When we write about problems, we automatically kickstart solutions. Journaling will also help you track your progress over time. We all have days when we think, "I've made no progress at all! I haven't done a thing!" When you feel like that, consult your Bliss Journal. Start by noting your thoughts and progress around the Bliss Keys you will find in chapter 3. I'll give you the first of these now.

Bliss Key #1: Slow Down

If you had a speedometer attached to your chest, what it would register when clocking the speed of your life? Are you going 80 miles an hour in a 35 zone? Pushing it into the red? Let your intuition guide you and write down the number. Now, think about what you would like the speed of your life to be. Write that down. If you long to go a leisurely 20 miles an hour but are now going 100, write that down. Next, think about three ways to slow down your life. They don't have to be big ways; they just have to be three things you can do to get more time and space into your life—perhaps dropping off the laundry at a cleaners instead of doing it yourself, or maybe organizing with neighbors to look after your kids once a week so you can have some private time, or getting your partner or the kids to take complete responsibility for your pet's walking and feeding for a week so that you can have some time to read or do yoga. Whatever slowing down means for you, implement at least one of these changes today and the other two in the following week.

YOUR OWN PERSONAL TIME GENERATOR

If you're in the grips of the adrenaline rush of too much to do and no time to do it, here's another way to literally create more time in your day. Make a grid like the one below. (Though this grid only goes to 10 A.M., make yours for however long your day is.) In twenty-minute increments, record how you use your time. Divide your time into four different categories: Time spent doing necessary work, either at a job or at home. Time used for yourself—for example, that 8 A.M. slot could be your morning shower. Time spent on your family—8:20 might be getting your kids their breakfast. And finally, time spent on miscellaneous items—9:40 might be you gossiping with coworkers as you start your day. Your activities may fall into more than one category at a time. For example, if you're at work but checking personal email you might place an X in two different columns, as in the 9:20 slot below, or even three, as in the 8:40 slot, where you might be driving your kids to school, yourself to work, and picking up a friend's dry-cleaning on the way. Take a look at how a typical morning of an overbooked woman can quickly stack up:

TIME OF DAY	WORK	SELF	FAMILY	MISC./OTHERS
8:00 A.M.		X	X	X
8:20 A.M.		X	X	
8:40 A.M.		X	X	X
9:00 A.M.	X			
9:20 A.M.	X	X		
9:40 A.M.	X			X
10:00 A.M.	X			X

Now, take a look at the 8 A.M. slot. You've woken up and maybe eaten breakfast. Simultaneously, other family members may be asking you to sew on a button or listen to a grievance, and you consent. You're also trying to give a few licks to a project your neighborhood committee has roped you into. Not one "my time" slot has nothing else competing with it—every time you give time to yourself, it's divided and unfocused. And you're probably not doing any of these tasks as well as you could with undivided attention. If you were to give up something in this scenario to gain more time for yourself, what would it be? You might choose to give up the committee work altogether or defer it to another time, for instance. What else could be moved, shifted, refocused, or delegated? Learn to think about your entire day this way. When you do, you gain back lost time.

When others eat into your time, it makes the tasks you have to do take longer. A prime example of this is when gossipy coworkers stop by your office to gab. You can dramatically shorten the time it takes to do necessary tasks simply by refusing to be interrupted. This is the time to get firm. Say, "I'll talk to you later," and make it stick. You'll soon begin seeing other ways to stop multitasking and generate more time and space to accomplish the things you need to get done in the time you have. And in so doing, your tasks will take half as long as they did when you multitasked.

ANALYZING YOUR TIME WASTERS

Fill a daily grid every day for a week. Identify both the categories that have the most checkmarks and the timeslots that have multiple checkmarks. These will be the areas to watch and play with rearranging. You'll want to:

1. Track your time for at least one full week; note how you spend your time and with whom. Use at least the four categories given above, plus any others you feel appropriate.

2. Create a Bliss Journal entry entitled "My Ideal Week." Write about what happens, who you are with, how you feel, and where you are.

3. Clarify your benchmark for success. How will you know when you've achieved your ideal week? What will you see and hear? How will you feel inside? This will not only help you recognize when you've arrived, it will also give you a good idea of where you're going.

And by the way, play is important! Allow yourself to be completely nonserious about generating more time. Remember that nothing is required of you. Knowing this, what will you do with your blocks of time? Can you allocate your precious personal resources differently? If you had one precious, extra hour a week, what would you do with it?

The universe hears and supports whatever you choose. Choose only nurturing things for your ideal week. Try a few of the mind shifts you've learned in this chapter.

Taking Your Life Back from Others

Your time gets taken by others, often with your full permission. "No way," you say? Nine times out of ten, people behave in patterns you train them to. When you don't say no and instead accept every project that comes along, others will continue to ask you to do such projects. When you don't set boundaries with your kids, partner, workmates, or others, they will expect you to conform to the way *they* view the world and do things for them accordingly. You don't have to allow this kind of behavior to continue unchecked. Instead, take charge—and in the process, take back your time and your life from draining relationships.

While it may be difficult in the beginning, it is well worth your time and energy to retrain others to act in ways that nurture and respect your space and sense of personal peace. They need to learn—from *you*—not to use you as their go-to person every single time there's a fire to put out, to respect that no means no. Sometimes you'll need to respond to their requests, but not always.

If you're thinking that it would be "bad" not to give as much of yourself to others as you currently do, then understand that by giving too much, you not only drain your own well, you also teach others not to be responsible for themselves and their needs. Now there's a thought. Kind of turns things around, doesn't it? The people who depend on you—particularly your children—need to know how to be responsible for themselves. Telling children no, that if they want help they have to come to you weeks before a project is due and not the night before, will help them learn to take responsibility. Once they get through calling you a meanie, your stance can lead to a fruitful discussion about how to plan better. And as those around you plan better, they'll bring you fires to fight less often—giving you even more time and space in your life. Similarly when your boss, neighbor, or church committee person comes to you for the third time in a row, put your foot down and politely explain to them that you've already done more than your share and will help again but can't take on every project every time.

If this seems impractical for you right now, just open yourself to the possibility of saying no and making it stick once a week. It may not be easy the first few times, but you can do it. The reward—more time, space, and sanity—is well worth the effort.

CHAPTER 2

Bliss and the Power of Belief

The most powerful tool in your bliss-making toolkit is the power of your beliefs. I cannot emphasize this enough. Your beliefs can free you or they can bind you. How many times have you heard "you can if you think you can"? It's actually true more often than you might think. Conversely, if you think you *can't* or *shouldn't* do something, you often won't be able to do it, no matter how much money, status, or power you have. Those of us who have unhealthily busy lives often believe we must stay on the treadmill of work, sweat, and exhaustion. We may believe, too, that the inevitable outcome of our lives is to be tired and frustrated—and that there is little help for it. It's a simple thing to recognize

This chapter relates to phases 2–4 of the Everyday Bliss Process, outlined on pages 10 and 11.

and believe that other options are possible, but most of us have never been taught how.

What you believe deeply influences what you are able to accomplish. Most of us have many more binding and blocking beliefs than beliefs that will enable us to live in bliss every day. Making important life changes starts with changing core beliefs. In this chapter, you'll learn what a belief is, how a belief originates, and most importantly, how to start "belief busting" unhelpful beliefs so that you embrace only those beliefs that support you and allow you to live in everyday bliss.

WHAT BELIEFS ARE AND HOW THEY CAN HELP OR HURT US

First let's examine what a belief is. A *belief* is a set of internal expectations that form as a result of a situation with strong impact. Beliefs are then codified and set into the subconscious by situations that reinforce this set of expectations. Negative beliefs might be, "I always mess up relationships" or "Holidays are always stressful." Positive beliefs, beliefs that uphold and encourage us, might be, "I'm good at math," "I'll find a way, I always do," "Help always comes at the right time for me," or "I am so very blessed and lucky." Both positive and negative beliefs form because we have experiences over and over again that reinforce the validity of our expectations.

Some developmental theorists believe that the belief structure that makes up our core personality is formed between birth and early to midchildhood. When we are that young, we cannot possibly understand the entirety of our world, and we do not have the many resources we will have as adults. Yet, unless we do something to change them, the beliefs we form in childhood still rule our lives twenty, thirty, forty years later. Fortunately, changing your mind isn't as difficult as it might appear. In fact, with a little practice, it's downright simple.

Whatever your beliefs about yourself, let's start with an initial reframing: know that you are okay, just as you are right now, warts and all. Really. You do not need to "fix" anything about yourself. Fixing implies brokenness. No matter how traumatic your life may have been, *you* are not broken. You are a complete and whole person and are here to live, love, and leave a vibrant legacy. If, however, there are holes in your life, they can be mended. If there's a lack in your life, it can be remedied. If there's something you really don't like about yourself, it can be changed. But get the idea that you need "fixing" to be a good and worthy person out of your head right now. You're fine. And help is here to make the less-than-perfect parts of your life bright and shiny again.

Kids, What Do They Know?
(As It Turns Out, a Lot!)

As children, our minds are active, inquisitive, and growing; we acquire beliefs—especially those that shape our core personality—from observing what is going on around us. Let's look at how childhood beliefs can affect us when we grow up. If a child is consistently told to hush when she speaks up, she may form the belief that speaking out leads to bad consequences—and come to the conclusion that she must not speak up for herself. As a result, as she grows into a woman, she won't speak up in her primary relationship, at work, or with friends.

Later, she may find it impossible to ask for a raise or better treatment in a relationship.

Beliefs may also be positive. We all have both positive and negative core beliefs about ourselves and our abilities. If the woman from the previous example had been praised when she spoke out as a child, she would have formed the beliefs that her words were worth hearing and that her opinion mattered. She would be able to ask for what she needed, refuse situations where she was called on to give too much, and place a high value on her own time and space.

It's very important to understand your core beliefs about yourself and your environment—not only the beliefs that bind you, but also those that support you and allow you to live the life you want. Supportive, positive beliefs can be leveraged to induce a sense of peace and calm in times of stress. Don't have many of these? Then we'll use the energy therapies we'll learn in the next few chapters to change negative beliefs about yourself into beliefs that support you.

BELIEF IN ACTION:
THE BELIEFS INVENTORY

Divide a sheet of paper in two. On one side, list the positive beliefs you have—beliefs that are affirming and encouraging. These beliefs can be about anything, from basic life issues to complex work functions. On the other side, list the negative beliefs you have—beliefs that either don't support you or work against you. If you're having difficulty thinking of things to put down, start a sentence with "I believe I …" and then fill in the blank. You're looking for beliefs about the abilities/talents or disabilities/dysfunctions of your core personality. The chart below offers a short example to consider, but you can go much further. In fact, keep going until you can't think of any more beliefs, positive or negative.

My Positive, Supportive Beliefs:	My Negative, Unsupportive Beliefs:
1. I can learn new things quickly.	1 I'm bad at speaking up for myself.
2. I have the skills to turn a nonproductive team around in two weeks flat.	2. I have poor boundaries; people walk all over me.
3. I am a kind and caring person and manager.	3. I can't say no or I'll look bad.
4. I attract friends easily.	4. I never behave correctly in social settings.
5. I am very good at scientific inquiry.	5. I shouldn't make more money than my parents.
6. I'm a great and supportive mom.	6. I have no right to be healthy and well.
7. I am a good caregiver for my parents.	7. I shouldn't rise above my station.
8. I can do anything I set my mind to.	8. I'll always date/marry losers.

Now, when you make your own lists, the first thing you may notice is that one of the columns is disproportionately longer than the other. Which is it for you? If your positive column is longer, great! You've got a lot of support within yourself. If your negative column is longer, that's great, too—now you recognize these beliefs and can work to change them.

If part of your life isn't as you want it, I encourage you to be of good cheer and simply commit to working on it. As the old saying goes: "If you're not working on yourself, you're not working." From your negative beliefs list, pick your three most important unsupportive beliefs. Choose no more than three! Work on no more than one or two of these top three at any one time. When you start to actually change your negative beliefs it can be tempting to rush through the entire list. But it's important to pace yourself: as you change energy connections in your body, you use energy; working on more than a few at any one time can become tiring.

Now, focus on whichever of your top three feels the least pleasant when you think of it.

Got your top limiting belief? Great. We're going to work this belief inside and out with Neurolinguistic Programming (NLP). NLP is a form of intentional energy therapy that focuses on how you code things in your mind; it helps you to literally break your own mental programming through changes in body movement, speech patterns, and eye movements. It's safe, fast, and effective. The following quick little exercise is my adaptation of the NLP Belief Change practice I learned from Robert Dilts.

THE WALKING BELIEF CHANGE EXERCISE

For this exercise, you'll need six sheets of paper and the space to ke five steps. Label your sheets of paper as below and lay them out on the floor:

1. Old Belief	2. Willing to Change	3. Dropping the Old Belief	4. Choosing a New Belief	5. Stepping into the New Belief	6. The New Old Story

1. Start with the top limiting belief you selected above. (Later, you can use this exercise with any belief you want.) Step onto the first piece of paper and say this old belief aloud. Notice how it feels to say it, how your body reacts. Ask yourself, "Is this true? How true is this?" Notice whether you still feel this old belief is entirely true. It may have diminished in the years since you first took it on.

2. Step onto the second piece of paper and affirm aloud that you are willing to change this belief. Think for a moment about what not having this belief will be like. Sometimes even negative beliefs can become precious to us, like old friends, and we may not want to let them go. Stand here until you can honestly say that you are willing to let this old belief go.

3. Step onto the third piece of paper and feel or see this old belief moving from wherever it lives inside of you to appear

in your hands. Give it a shape, perhaps a color. What does it look like? How does it feel in your hands? When you're ready, you're going to put this belief into what we call the Museum of Old Beliefs.

See a thick, bulletproof glass museum case in front of you; hear it creak slightly as you open it. As you place your old belief inside the case, thank it for what it was trying to do for you. Beliefs come into being to help us in some way—usually to keep us from getting hurt. Even though this old belief no longer works for you, it once had a purpose. By thanking it, you're tying up the last loose ends and letting go. Now close the case. Feel, hear, or see the lid fall heavily shut, sealing the old belief inside.

Turn away from the case and move your eyes in the pattern of an infinity symbol. Trace this sideways figure eight three times with your eyes and then draw in a big, deep breath. Slowly blow every last bit of this breath out. These processes will help work the very last bits of that old belief out of you.

4. Step out of the Museum of Old Beliefs and onto the next sheet of paper. Think about what new, positive, and you-enhancing belief you would like to choose to embrace in

the place of this old belief. Your new belief should be an opposite of the old belief that bolsters the area that was previously undermined. See, feel, and even hear how this new belief will affect your life.

5. Step onto the fifth piece of paper, the place of the new belief. Say the new belief aloud to yourself three times in a strong voice. Phrase the belief a bit differently each time to help reinforce it. For example: "I believe I am worthy of love. I deeply and completely believe I am worthy of love. I absolutely accept that I am worthy of love." Feel this empowering new belief sink deep down within you. Enjoy how it feels.

6. Step onto the last piece of paper and tell yourself *what it has been like* to have this empowering new belief. Tell yourself your own life story in brief, from birth onwards, as if you'd had this belief all your life—as if you'd *always* been smart, strong, worthy of love, or whatever new belief you chose. And for the key incidents connected to the old belief, tell yourself how differently those situations went, having this new belief. For example, if you were put down at school and never stood up for yourself, revisit one of these incidents and tell yourself how marvelously well you stood up for yourself and how the other kids respected you for it. (This isn't just telling yourself pretty stories—you are literally recoding your neurology for success by doing this.)

Add body movement as you experience how differently this new belief makes you feel. Take three or four minutes to dance, stretch, or do whatever feels right for you. Be sure to bring yourself fully up to the present in your new old story. Finish with a sentence or two about how your new belief will impact your future next month, six months, and a year from now. Envision these future successes. Reach out and gather all of these lovely visions to you. Hold them gently over your heart; allow this empowering new belief structure to sink deep down within you.

7. Describe the future you have seen in your Bliss Journal.

Rest. You are finished. Once you get good at it, a Walking Belief Change will only take you a matter of minutes. Start on the big hairy unsupportive beliefs first—those beliefs that have dogged you throughout your life. As you change in this process, your body will relax and your mind will settle into a peaceful state. Enjoy the changes that will sprout up in your life—you've just reprogrammed yourself for greater relaxation, success, and bliss.

THE TOXIC POWER OF NEGATIVE BELIEF STORIES (A.K.A. "B.S.")

After I emerged from years of paralysis, I felt a tremendous need to apologize for being slow, overweight, and lacking in strength. I did this by telling the story of my broken back to everyone I met, elaborating on both how much I had suffered—and was still suffering—and how hard

I was working on my recovery. My client Eva, a VP of engineering at a computer software company, had a similar experience. After a car accident led to facial reconstructive surgery, Eva dwelt on her suffering and the hard work she'd done in speech therapy, as she felt this somehow legitimized her other deficiencies and excused her for not being what society said she should be. She reported feeling greatly diminished by the entire experience and constantly feeling like she had to justify her slightly slurred speech to those who didn't know her medical history. She, like I, had the belief that she was somehow less than those around her. Our need to be known with dignity—and not just as the external wrapper others saw—drove both of us to tell our story again and again. Unfortunately, as long as we kept our energy invested in the negative beliefs that went with our stories, we prevented ourselves from forming new and supportive beliefs.

Thanks to brilliant, caring friends and an extraordinarily dedicated yoga teacher, I realized that I wasn't simply a broken-back story and got on with living my life. Eva had a similar realization and turned her life around by reidentifying with a long list of descriptors that said more about who she really was as a person. Near the end of that list was the descriptor of someone who had, incidentally, long ago had facial surgery. This was a much more realistic way to live and began attracting the kinds of positive situations Eva desired—situations that living in the story had previously driven off.

We are, in great part, the sum of our experiences. A belief story (or "B.S.") has its place both in our initial integration of traumatic experiences and as part of our personal history. But when a framework of negative beliefs becomes the defining feature of personal identity, our strength is sapped, and our efforts to regain normality are thwarted. In this case, a negative belief story becomes a *toxic belief*. A toxic belief is a strong position you hold, whether you're aware of it or not, that keeps you from living a healthy, happy life. It's the little gremlin whispering in your mind, "You can't do that; you never could!" "Are you crazy?" "People will think you're stupid if you try!" or "Best to stay quiet and avoid being seen as a fool." These and similar phrases are the work of the toxic-belief gremlin. Its voice might sound like a parent, critical teacher, snobby workmate, or even your own. Nothing quite lays you as low as this voice, for this is the one voice you cannot walk away from. It's the one voice that will always be with you—unless you actively do something about it. The following short exercise will teach you how to address this voice by getting to the heart of the negative beliefs that may be defining you.

ARTICULATING YOUR STORY

Speaking of toxic beliefs, what's *your* belief story? You may never have had a catastrophic accident, but if you're telling others and yourself the same things year after year about why you're not where you want to be, you have a belief story. Where does this story fit into your life? How attached to it are you? How much do you defend your story's right to exist? Everyone has a history; some part of your history probably pulls you to relive your own personal pain, again and again.

Spend some time in meditative reflection on each of these questions, and allow the main elements of your belief story to surface. You want only the highlights of the story, not a blow-by-blow account. For example: "I'm just a poor kid from the wrong side of the tracks; that's why I've never been able to obtain anything better than a low-end management job." Or "I'm never going to be good at math, so I'll always keep making money and losing it, no matter what I do." Or "My mom chose a bad husband, her mom chose a bad husband, and so did I. I'm doomed to never have a good mate—it's in my blood." In five to ten sentences write these main elements down, either here or in your Bliss Journal, to help get them out of your head. Once you have your main stories written down, you can transfer the negative beliefs they contain to your Shadow List and work on them with the Walking Belief Change process or other energy therapies you'll learn shortly.

A belief story, while potentially toxic, is also a sacred and beautiful signpost of your life. Spend a few moments cherishing your story. Now, contemplate what it would be like to let that belief story go, never to tell it in the old familiar way again. If this brings up emotions for you, record them in your Bliss Journal. If this triggers emotions or thoughts you've never encountered before, also note them on your Shadow List. You'll work on these later. For right now, just document your belief story.

Mine Your Story, Then Lose It

Like many people, I became tired of my dysfunctional story in time and came to the realization that the universe had far greater in store for me than I could ever imagine. And then came a long line of spiritual teachers, including Joseph Campbell, Wayne Dyer, and Eckhart Tolle, whose sage wisdom bade me to let my belief story go in order to open up to the richer and more rewarding life that I desired. I encourage you to do the same, scary though it may be.

There is, however, great wisdom to be found in each of our belief stories. Take some time to think about the wisdom you've gained from living your belief story—what skills and talents you've obtained and what situations have occurred or people you've met. Then think about who you will be without your story to fall back on. It may be difficult at first to imagine living your life without your belief story, but from now on, you have a completely clean slate and permission to dream.

Now that you have an idea of what it might be like to drop the identity your belief story has imposed on you, practice living these insights daily.

DAILY PROTECTION SPHERE

If you're feeling a little raw and exposed without your belief story—or any time—do this simple exercise to form a protective energy bubble around yourself. I and many other energy coaches incorporate this exercise into our daily routines to keep our body/mind energy running as cleanly and healthily as possible.

Whether it's night or day where you presently are, the sun is shining somewhere in the world. Focus on the sun and draw its golden light inside yourself. Fill your body to the bursting point with this golden light. Revel in how good, cleansing, and purifying it feels. When you're so full that you cannot hold any more, allow the golden light to flow outward from your body to create a bubble or sphere that surrounds you and extends several feet in every direction. Don't forget to let the light flow behind you, above you, under your feet (extending into the earth below you), and to each side. Let the light flow outward until your personal sphere feels completely full.

This sphere protects your personal energy at all times; it is inviolable. You alone determine what energy comes in and what energy goes out. If you're feeling particularly vulnerable, envision the outer edge of your sphere hardening into polished, hardened steel. Make this shiny outer shell as thick as you want. This is where foreign energies stop and will by default be reflected back to their givers. Your energies stay in; others' stay out. You may choose to let someone's energies through or give another some of your own energy, but this is your conscious choice. Breathe very deeply into your center and let the visualization gently dissipate. You are now fully protected. Renew this protection at least three times during a day for maximum effectiveness.

We Can Do Anything We Set Our Minds To

My mother repeated the above words to me in some form or another at least eight or ten times a day, throughout my life. For various reasons that seem silly to me now, I maintained the unsupportive belief that she was wrong. Now, decades later, I know how wise she really was. We can really, seriously, do anything we set our minds to. Choosing to leave our belief stories behind and strike out boldly without them takes guts and determination, but the rewards are great. What can you accomplish without your story? After years of speech therapy—which she'd initially refused, thinking she'd never be able to speak normally again—Eva has progressed from being barely understood to achieving her longtime bliss goal: being the lead singer in a local rock band. Because I chose to stop defining myself by my broken-back story and accept that boundless health could be mine, I can dance again.

Letting go of a belief story can be a protracted experience. Hold tight to the beliefs that strengthen you. As I said before, with enough determination and belief, there's absolutely nothing you can't do. If you believe strongly that you can, you will. If you believe you can create wellness and everyday bliss, they will be yours. And without the interference of toxic belief stories, they will be yours all the quicker.

Meditation Point

What is your belief story making it seem impossible for you to accomplish? Is it finding more time in your day for you? Getting the housework all done while juggling reports for work? Trying to get your toddler to eat her spinach without a range war? Whatever it is, consider the situation and say slowly but firmly to yourself the following precept of Neurolinguistic Programming: "There is no failure, only feedback." Now, say it again. One more time. Mean it. Analyze the feedback you're getting as if you were a scientist in a lab. What can you do with this valuable data that will enable you to proceed in a more focused and reasoned manner?

Drop your toxic belief story, step out the door, and explore the amazing new life that awaits you. Check all "shoulds, "coulds," and "oughts" at the door. Listen to your body and to your heart—they will tell you what to do. Keep listening. What supportive, nurturing, new beliefs will you choose to take on today?

Abundance and Scarcity

Bound up in our belief stories are various individual beliefs about what we can and can't do and should and shouldn't have in our lives. These beliefs determine whether we live our lives from a place of abundance or one of scarcity and lack. Kim George, director of the AQ Institute (www.coachingintogreatness.com), has been researching contrasting belief systems; she generously shared her results with me. Kim has identified seven illusions as the primary sources of scarcity thinking in people's lives as well as seven corresponding aptitudes that lead to abundance thinking. Kim has written extensively about this in her book *Coaching Into Greatness* (2006), but I'd like to share just one of these illusions here: the "illusion of struggle."

Most of us have grown up with the idea that struggling is a necessary, even virtuous part of life. This is incorrect. Struggling is not only overrated, but entirely unnecessary. In fact, struggling can be a primary Bliss Blocker. You'll learn more about this in the next chapter, when we discuss the Law of Attraction, but suffice to say, you can begin to extricate yourself from the illusion of struggle by embracing its opposite aptitude of abundance, self-expression. When we are fully self-expressed, we live for the excitement of just getting up every morning, and we do things for the sheer joy of doing them. When we are fully self-expressed, we are open to receive the many gifts the universe offers us and to accept them with deep gratitude. We divest of stuff, complexity, and intrigue. Life becomes simple, basic, and as such, beautifully rewarding and deeply fulfilling. This blissful, abundant state is similar in some interesting ways to psychologist Mihaly Csikszentmihalyi's "flow" (1991).

Meditation Point

Where in your life do you struggle? What complexities and intrigues are there in your life that you can release? What material possessions or stuff can you divest yourself of, either by selling items, recycling or trashing them, or, better yet, giving them away? If you say, "But I need them!" ask yourself the time-honored clarity question: "Is that really true?" and try to remember the last time you used these items. If it was over a year ago, consider letting them go. To achieve true bliss, simplify, simplify, simplify.

YOUR LIFE MISSION

To create the life of your dreams and banish the doleful trio of busyness, exhaustion, and frustration from your daily experience, you need to determine your *life mission*. Your life mission is a major overriding life goal. When you live your life in accordance with your life mission, you automatically feel happier and more fulfilled. Living at odds with your life mission invites energy drain, clouded thinking, fatigue, and a host of other unhappy symptoms.

Your life mission could be anything. Your mission could be deeply spiritual: to memorize your religion's holy book and teach its wisdom. It could be creative: to live your life expressing a particular kind of art, dance, or other creative endeavor. It could be focused on family: to be the best mom you can and raise amazing human beings. It could be local: to enlarge your community's open space to a certain acreage. Or it could be global: to create a whole new kind of communication forum between nations that allows everyone to feel valued and heard. It could be similar to any one of these examples or something altogether different. Your life mission should be something that excites you and makes you feel happy when you consider spending your life in its fulfillment.

One woman who fully embraced her life mission was Mother Teresa. Her mission was to give comfort to the poor, which she did every day of her life. And although she lived in squalor while doing so, fulfillment of her mission brought her great joy. Closer to home are women like my client Mara, a doctor on the board of directors of a healthcare research company. Her life mission is to give every person in the United States access to affordable healthcare. She is fulfilling this mission by getting reasonably priced healthcare plans into the hands of employers, so employees don't have to make painful choices about the care they receive. Secondarily, as a proponent of alternative medicine, she has a mission to make sure the plans her company sells cover things like acupuncture and chiropractic care. Despite company resistance, Mara has successfully fought to make this a reality. It is an ongoing mission that gives her deep joy.

What do you most desire to do in the world before you leave it? What will give you supreme joy to do? Use your life mission as a signpost—it will direct you to everything you want for yourself. Seeing your life mission in front of you is like viewing a goal that has already come to fruition. Constantly check your choices against your life mission; ask yourself, "Is this activity getting me closer to achieving my mission?" If an activity makes you feel happy and fulfilled, then the activity is necessary and appropriate for you. On the other hand, any commitment, activity, or relationship that prevents you from fulfilling your mission is a Bliss Blocker and therefore something you shouldn't spend your precious time on.

CHAPTER 3

Become Overwhelmingly Attractive: Attracting What You Want

*W*hile our situations are all different, the reason we get out of bliss and caught up in busy, tiring, and frustrating lifestyles is often the same: attention to the wrong things. While paralyzed, I focused on how desperate and problematic my life was—to excess. I moaned and griped about it. I convinced myself that no one had ever had it so hard. As a consequence, things went from bad to worse—because that's what I was focusing on: how *bad* things were! Energy flows where attention

This chapter relates to phase 5 of the Everyday Bliss Process, outlined on page 11.

goes. It's as simple as that. Thus, when you focus on how busy and tired you are, you get more of the same.

Does this sound familiar to you? If so, good—you probably already have a good idea as to which beliefs to start changing and which thoughts and attitudes to work on. If not, the basic premise is that like attracts like; you attract what you most often think about. (If you saw the movie *The Secret* then you know that your thoughts in large part govern what you experience in life.) We call this the *Law of Attraction*. When I was first introduced to this idea, it wasn't called the Law of Attraction; it was considered just good common sense. My grandmother Mimi summed it up nicely:

> *If you don't want something in your life, honey, then make*
> *yourself into a magnet for what you do what. A magnet attracts*
> *the same thing it's made of—and so can you, by thinking and*
> *praying about what you want every day. When you think about*
> *how bad things are all the time, you get more of the bad. Be*
> *grateful, give thanks for what you've got, and love the life you*
> *have. That's how to get what you want!*

This is the same advice my mother gave me every time I came home with a skinned knee, a broken heart, or gripes about school or work. It's what most of us were told in some way or another growing up, usually couched as "Say your prayers and be thankful." Like kids everywhere, most of us probably discounted this advice from our elders. I sure did. It took me another twenty years before I realized that the wisdom of my elders was actually also the way to everyday bliss.

CREATING YOUR OWN BLISS MAGNET

If you focus exclusively on what you have to be grateful for, on what you most deeply need and desire, your life will begin to change for the better. It may take a number of months and a great deal of focused concentration, but it will happen. Letting go of not just your belief story, but also whatever no longer fits your life or is painful, and focusing instead on what can be, is just the catalyst you need to attract what you want in life.

But what about areas in your life where you're stuck? The first step is to let go of what cannot be changed, what can only be endured. This is a pivotal step in the transformation of misery into bliss. In order to become irresistibly attractive to that we most deeply desire, we sometimes have to let go of the old and instead gather in new ideas, people, and information. As my clients and I have discovered, the formula for attracting bliss is extremely simple:

1. Don't focus on your pain, but don't ignore it either. *Do* work to improve whatever is undesired in your life.

2. Give great and continuing gratitude for what you *do* have.

3. Focus on what you want with single-minded intensity. Create a new story for your life. Imagine this new story. Make it as big, bold, and Technicolor as you possibly can. See it. Feel it. Taste it. Smell it. Wrap your arms, your legs, your body around it. Enjoy how delicious it is to slow down and live a new and more positive story.

4. Dream forward in time—experience how differently people react to you in your new life. Revel in their positive, uplifting words to you. See, feel, and hear your new life multiple times a day. Dream it into existence. (Try it; it actually works!)

5. Repeat multiple times daily until manifested. That's it!

Having a beautiful, blissful life is this simple. If you want to attract relaxation, supreme health, or whatever makes up your definition of bliss, then, just as my grandmother sagely advised, that's what you need to concentrate on.

CREATING YOUR TREASURE MAP

A *treasure map* is a meditation icon that can both help you to create your desired future by fixing it in your attention, and cheer you on as you work to bring this new life into being. Consider the life you've dreamed into being above. Flesh this picture out as much as you can. Take careful note of your surroundings. See how you look and what you're wearing. Think about who you'll hang out with, what you'll say, what others will say to you, where you'll be geographically, what important events will happen to you, and so on.

Once you have a strong mental picture in place, make a physical picture. Find images that represent the different elements of your new life and collage them together in a way that is beautiful to you. This treasure map will irresistibly draw you toward these very things. Place it in your personal altar space and meditate on this treasure map daily. As your experience and preferences change, so can your map. The more you focus your attention (and hence your energy) on your treasure map, the more swiftly you will draw its contents toward you.

KEEPING YOUR OWN WELL FULL

If you're in a position of responsibility that keeps you tremendously busy and drains you dry, you must focus on taking care of *you* first. Remember the airline safety lecture: put on your own oxygen mask first, then help others. If you don't take care of yourself first, you may not be there to take care of anyone else. As women, we're often socially conditioned to care for others first, which can make this precept particularly hard to embrace.

The truth is, most of the time, we don't take care of ourselves first. Most of us concentrate on how miserable we feel, how fat we look, how broke we are, how the person next door really bugs us with their loud music, how we just can't stand our job. This doesn't get us happiness, a fit body, more money, a quiet home, or a great new job. When we think like this, we only attract more of the same—more misery, more weight, more financial woes, more neighbor troubles, more bad job karma. Still, it can be tough to break out of these unhealthy ruts—just like tire tracks in an old dirt road, these mental patterns are so deep that we often fall into them instinctively, without thinking.

So, if we attract what we think about, how do we break the bonds of negative thinking in order to get with the program? First, you need to recognize your preprogrammed negative thinking; then you need to rechannel it. Make it a game: try to catch yourself whenever you're in a pity party. And when you do find yourself focusing on the negative, try one of the following three instant Negativity Erasers:

1. Hit the stop button. Go ahead and tell that thought to *stop*! Use your index finger to hit an imaginary stop button in the air. Next, gently tap your index finger to your palm a few times while you think of the *opposite* condition— what you would like to have happen. This will help you re-route your mind away from those old negativity ruts and into positive ones.

2. Say, either aloud or to yourself, "Cancel, cancel!" Immediately replace the negative thought you're cancel-ing with a positive thought that gives you great pleasure and moves you toward the life you want. Spend a few moments reveling in how delicious this new thought is.

3. Stand up, say "Stop!" and step to the left or right. In your new location luxuriate in whatever you would rather think about instead. Feel a smile spread across your face. Alternate between thinking your pleasant new thoughts and feeling the smile. Shift your mental focus back and forth three or four times as you feel your smile grow larger. After you've done this maneuver for ten or so different instances of negative thinking, all you'll need do is notice the negative thought and quickly step sideways. That should be enough to trigger your mind to remember this little program, thus stopping the negativity and shifting to positivity instead.

THINKING ONLY THE BEST THOUGHTS

So, what kind of positive thoughts is it best to concentrate on? I'm glad you asked, because thoughts about how much you love ice cream or enjoy looking at the new hottie at work aren't what we're talking about. Get out the Bliss List you made in chapter 1. Take a good long look at the items on this list. If you haven't yet done so, shortlist your top five items, numbering them in order of importance to you. (You can put more than five possible treats on your shortlist, but keep this list small when you start out so that you have a manageable block to concentrate on.) Note what specific bliss goal you are seeking when you implement these items.

As you do Negativity Erasers, you'll replace negative thoughts with thoughts about items on your Bliss List shortlist. Let's say "daily meditation" is the first item on your list, with "general relaxation" as its specific bliss goal. As you use one of the Negativity Eraser techniques described above, switch from your negative thought to seeing and feeling yourself in meditation. Notice how extremely relaxed you are. Notice how all those tense little places in your mind and body smooth out as you meditate to feel easy, light, and calm. Why, just thinking about how wonderful it is to meditate relaxes you. Feel a smile spread slowly across your face as your mind and body let go. That's right. You're there—and it only took a few seconds.

Now, consciously notice how much nicer it is to think about meditating (or whatever item you chose) than the negative thought you were previously thinking. What the heck *were* you thinking about? Can't remember? Is that negative getting a little fuzzy? A lot fuzzy? Good.

You've done it. The next time a negative thought rears its ugly head, slot thoughts about item #2 from your Bliss List shortlist into whatever Negativity Eraser you choose, and so on. If you're like I was, you'll have hundreds of moments every day to practice this. The more you practice, the more you'll create a vortex of energy that draws bliss inexorably toward you. The more you weed out negative thoughts, the more you'll make yourself a magnet for what you really *do* want.

It may be difficult initially to believe this will work. Keep at it! Perseverance is the key to getting anywhere in life, including turning yourself into a bliss magnet. But what should you do when the process appears to only kind of work or not work at all? Let's say you've been consistently replacing negative thoughts with wonderful thoughts about meditating, but you're still not attracting the results you want. Instead, every day, when you reach your appointed meditation time, the laundry or dishes "need" to be done, your emails "need" to be read, or some other task "needs" to be taken care of—until meditation time is long over and the rest of your day's agenda has taken over. "Darn!" you think to yourself, "I'll do better tomorrow!" And maybe you will, but the fact is, it can be difficult to maintain a meditation practice—or practice of any other Bliss List item—with a full list of to-do's waiting in the wings.

I'd like to encourage you to treat yourself with great and expansive kindness. Be sweet to yourself. Don't get down on yourself for not accomplishing items on your to-do list. Be kind about perceived failures. The old saying that you catch more flies with honey than vinegar has merit. If you are kind to yourself, you'll be much more attractive—both to yourself and to the people and situations you wish to draw into your life. Remember: "There is no failure, only feedback."

When you "fail" at a task, all that's really happened is that you've found an approach that leads to results you didn't expect. In academia, this is called research—and so it is in your life. Relabel failure as "new evidence gathered" and celebrate the fact that you've found another piece of the equation of your life.

ATTRACT BY SAYING NO

As we discussed in chapter 1, it's important to know when to say no. Make a habit of saying no—without explanation—to roughly a third of the requests that you would normally say yes to automatically. When you try to explain, people have a tendency to use your explanation to try and convince you that you are being selfish. Yes, you are being selfish, but selfish in a very good way. Keep this kind of selfish in your vocabulary, because it means taking care of yourself first so that you can take care of others better later. To do this, you'll have to first train others not to continue to expect the selfless giving they may have received from you in the past. This doesn't mean you're being nasty to them, and it doesn't mean you're not supporting those who ask you to do things for them. What it means is that you're filling your own cup first. And filling your own cup first is very, very attractive to those things that you want in life. Filling your own cup first tells bliss: "I'm ready for you! Come on in!" Bliss will respond to such an attractive force by coming into your life in ever-increasing amounts.

A Phenomenal Woman, Just Like You

Susan Foster was one of only ten civilians sent to the elite and nearly all-male U.S. Army War College, along with colonels being groomed for higher military service. Her performance there garnered her a promotion to the Pentagon in 2000. On September 11, 2001, she was just one floor above where terrorists crashed American Airlines Flight 77 into the Pentagon. Here, in her own words, is what happened:

I was in my boss's office with my employee, briefing [my boss] for the day. Somebody ran in and told us that the World Trade Center had been hit by a plane. We knew after hearing about the second plane that it was some kind of terrorist attack. I'd just said, "I'm surprised it hasn't happened here," when all of a sudden we saw this huge, huge flash of brilliant light. Then a fireball ran down the side of the building and the whole building started shaking and falling in. For a moment, my boss, my employee, and I sat there stunned.... I thought we were being bombed—it never occurred to me that we had been hit by another plane. My boss then screamed at us to get out. We ran into the hall, but fire was already coming up the stairwell. [Through all of the smoke,] I saw this incredibly bright blue light, took in a deep breath, and just kept walking toward it until I was out. Although I had a little bit of smoke in my lungs, I didn't even have a run in my stockings or a piece of glass in me—even though we'd been sitting right by glass windows that shattered.

Later, my boss told me the plane had come in right beneath where we were standing, impacting the first and second floor. Those people were gone—they've never been found. Once you hear that, you think, "Why did I survive when they didn't?" And then you think,... I've got to do something with my life. Life is never quite the same again.

This incident and those that followed started a process that totally rearranged Susan's priorities. She examined the negative habits and beliefs she held and actively worked from a place of deep gratitude to rearrange her life to attract peace and calm.

"What came out of that as important," Susan told me, "was that being able to get up in the morning is a gift. Being able to be with family and friends is a gift. And even if everything else goes away, as long as you've got that you're okay. Every day above ground is a good day." Susan finds herself a softer person now, with more empathy and an awareness that life is too short to harbor stress, ill feelings, or perfectionism. She says, "I'm kinder to myself now. I take lots of breaks and I don't allow others to overload me with work. I ask them to prioritize their needs from me. And I literally sit down and share with them what's going to get done and what isn't."

Hear that? It's okay to tell people, "These things are falling off the list." In fact, when you're dealing with people who are perfectionistic or driven, being crystal clear about priorities is absolutely the right tack to take. If someone is very demanding of your time, give them a choice of ten minutes now or half an hour later. If you're given one too many projects, say, "I'll do that project or the other one, but not both." What you communicate when you set boundaries like this is that your time is very valuable. The universe will respond by giving you more quality time.

"For me," says Susan, "bliss is contentment about who I am and where I'm going and what I have.... Bliss is sitting and looking at an ocean, living every minute to the fullest, enjoying every day. I want to be able to find happiness in whatever I'm doing, all day. It's taking a walk with my husband. It's having a good book to read. It's coming to the end of the day and phoning friends to reconnect. It's feeling like I made a difference."

While Susan's story is quite extraordinary, she is only one of many who chose to take the events of 9/11 as a wake-up call and upgrade their lives as a result. If you haven't yet gotten a wake-up call, consider the fact that you're reading this book to be it. The alarm is ringing. And this time hitting the snooze button won't work—it's time to get busy being good to yourself!

A THIRTY-DAY SELF-LOVE CHALLENGE

If your schedule is overbooked, I challenge you to refuse all external projects for thirty days. Only attend to the needs of those in your immediate family—and only when refusing to do so will upset your relationship dynamic. If your children need help with their homework, then of course, go ahead and help them. If your ailing parent needs a ride to the doctor, of course, do it. We need to be good to our families. But beyond this, discipline yourself to say no. If this is difficult for you, know that it's a twenty-first-century survival skill you *must* learn in order to achieve bliss as an everyday experience.

Learning to say no is one of the most extremely effective and far-reaching forms of self-love there is. What you are telling your inner self is: "I love you enough to pay attention to you exclusively." How often do we tell ourselves that? Not often. But we should—it's good for the body, mind, *and* spirit.

Ditch the Explanations

Enjoy the good feelings and mental freedom that arise from having more space in your schedule. Be prepared to be firm with those whom you are reeducating to depend less on you. Remember, it's important not to explain. It's none of their business, and you don't owe anyone any form of explanation. Explanations give the other party ammunition to draw the conversation out unproductively and make you feel guilty. Don't give in. Here are a few ways to say no politely but without explaining yourself:

Them: "Oh, surely you can bake a few brownies for the PTA fundraiser."

You: "Thanks for thinking of me, but I just don't have the time right now. Perhaps next semester."

Them: "We'd like you to host the society's monthly meeting in your office's conference room this Thursday. I'll just put you down, and you can email us which room to go to."

You: "It's a great honor to be asked, but I'm going to have to pass it on to someone else as I'm not able to host the meeting this time. Please do ask me again another time, though."

Them: *(tugging on your shirt)* "But I'm your brother/sister/best friend from college! You have to help me out! I'm serious, this is the last time I'll ever ask, but you just *gotta*...."

You: "I know I'm usually there for you, but right now I just can't be. I'd be happy to lend you my phone to call someone else though." Hand them your phone, cross your arms, and try not to stare too pointedly. Conversation over.

Refuse to reengage with persistent whiners: "I appreciate you need help and I usually do help you out, but as I said, it's just not convenient" or "I simply don't have the time." Just keep repeating this phrase. On the second or third go-round, most people will get it and cease asking.

If you want to keep lines of communication open, you may want to take a friendlier tack:

Them: "But *why*? What could be more important than your child's schooling?"

You: "Like I said, I just don't have the time right now. I do intend to come to the fundraiser though, and look forward to supporting the PTA. See you at the event!" And, with a cheery wave of your hand, off you go.

The preceding two examples are for the freeloading relatives, coworkers, and old friends who always lean on you. They fall into the category of the 20 percent of people who suck away 80 percent of your time and energy. Giving your time and energy to them once in a while is fine, but the expectation that you'll always do so needs to be sharply cut off. You are not their personal pool of energy to dip into whenever they feel like it. You have your own life to tend to. Cutting people like this off, gently but firmly, is the kindest thing you can do—for both of you. It encourages everyone to take responsibility for their own lives and energy. Be busy when they call or visit, change the locks if you've unwisely given out keys, and have an answer like the above ready in case they fall into begging or whining. Don't give in. Stand firm.

66

It Doesn't Have to Be Perfect, It Just Has to Be Done

It's pivotal that people learn for themselves. How many times have you wanted to "save someone the trouble" or done something because "if you want something done right, you have to do it yourself"? When you do everything for others, you both stress yourself incredibly and deprive the other people of their right to learn. This goes for children as much as it does for our partners, social relationships, and work relationships. Remember: things often don't have to be 100 percent perfect; they just have to be done. We have a saying in the coaching world: "Done = done." Think about it.

Blissful Attraction Secret
LEVERAGE THE POWER OF GROUPS

One of the secrets to attracting bliss is leveraging the power of local masterminding. Club together with other parents in your neighborhood to look after each other's children at least one or two days a week, or with other solo entrepreneurs to split the costs of a personal assistant. Join a walking group to get out of the house or an entrepreneurs' network to get business problems solved creatively. Whatever your work or home situation, there are others in your area in the same boat. Find them. Work together to help each other achieve everyday bliss. (In chapter 9, you'll find a guide to setting up your own Everyday Bliss Mastermind Group.)

BLISS BLOCKERS AND BLISS KEYS

The rest of this chapter is dedicated to Bliss Blockers—those things that literally hide bliss from you—and Bliss Keys, keys that can open doors to your having more peace, relaxation, and fulfillment in life. Each of these keys features a quick shift or action you can take to leverage yourself out of the doldrums and onto the path you want.

Bliss Blocker #1: Living at Warp Speed

As we discussed in chapter 1, if you live your life at warp speed, one day you'll crash and burn. Remember: Superwoman doesn't exist except in fiction.

Bliss Key #1: Slow Down

Slow way down. Really. If you find this idea painful, you, like most of us in the West, are probably addicted to adrenaline. To beat this addiction, drive the speed limit, drink only decaf and pure water, avoid harmful drugs altogether, and cultivate the daily practice of setting yourself apart from the world in prayer, meditation, or simple quiet reflection.

Bliss Blocker #2: Rigidity

Rigid attitudes, rigid routines that "cannot" be broken, and even physical, muscular rigidity (indicating a high-stress lifestyle) can all prevent you from living in everyday bliss.

When we are rigid, we aren't able to tolerate situations or reactions outside the narrow bandwidth of our tightly-defined parameters. This puts us in line for disappointment, frustration, and—sometimes—angry confrontations with those we perceive to have blocked us. Take a look at where rigidity might exist in your life. Is there someone you know who "never does it right"—the way *you* would do things? Children and partners are particularly good teachers of this lesson. How many times have you taken over a task from a child or partner, muttering under your breath, "If you want something done right, you have to do it yourself"? This is a prime indicator of rigidity. Remember, you're a sleuth now, on the trail of your own Bliss Blockers. How many places (including your own muscles!) can you find where rigidity exists?

Bliss Key #2: Flexibility

The element of a situation that has the most flexibility will control that situation. Be the flexible element in all situations. Learn how to be flexible, even if this initially requires spending great amounts of energy. That which flexes, endures. As we learn to flex with the strong tides of our lives, we find bliss where only fear existed previously. When a storm thunders into your life, bend like the trees. As you progress through the Everyday Bliss Process, you'll find that the more clarity you gain, the more those storms lessen—until finally they disappear altogether.

Bliss Blocker #3: Never Having Enough

This is the feeling that you will never have enough, do enough, be enough; that time, money, opportunities, and resources are slipping away from you.

Bliss Key #3: Know That There Will Always Be Enough

What is meant for you can never be lost. Keep your eyes open, but rest assured that if you don't catch the first instance of an opportunity, it will come around again. It may be wearing a different face or describe itself differently, but it will come around again.

Bliss Blocker #4: Living Unconsciously

When you don't bring your conscious presence to your life, you end up in ruts that may not support the blissful life you truly want to life. Life on autopilot is not "living."

Bliss Key #4: Stay in the Present Moment

The body is your primary means of staying in the present. When doubt, weirdness, or trouble comes into your life, put your hand on your heart and pay deep attention only to its beating and the rhythm of your breath. Allow the sensations of your body to bring you back to the here and now.

In his landmark consciousness-raising book, *The Power of Now* (1999), spiritual teacher Eckhart Tolle explains that the present is the only timeframe that can truly be said to exist in human consciousness. Tolle advocates staying in the present moment as a cure for stress—especially when bad things threaten to ruin a day. In the present moment, there is nothing really wrong. Really. Ask yourself: "Is anything wrong in the *now*?" Take stock of the present: "I'm breathing, my belly is full, I have clothes on my back and a roof over my head...." You may have a bad marriage, crappy job, debts, or a disease, but in the present moment, you're just fine. Make it a practice to bring yourself back into the now, day by day, minute by minute, moment by moment.

Bliss Blocker #5: Getting Lost in Minutiae

We are assailed by hundreds of thousands of discrete pieces of information daily. We cannot possibly take them all in. Instead, we must make choices about what we wish to pay attention to. Getting upset about the small things—minutiae like crumbs on the floor, for instance—is not a worthy use of your time (unless of course, you're a professional house cleaner).

Bliss Key #5: Focus on What's Most Important

Focus only on whatever are, right now, your top three most important things. These aren't your goals for all time; they're what's important today to pay attention to, to work with, to see accomplished. What can you do to further these three most important things? Anything not connected to these top three—unless it's a hair-raising emergency—is a distracter, aiming to steal your time. Don't let it!

The old-timers are right: ignorance is bliss. Choose to be ignorant of the unimportant crumbs so that you may pay attention to what really matters. When you truly let go of the need to have all the minutiae of your life in perfect alignment, you will achieve a level of bliss you wouldn't believe possible.

Bliss Blocker #6: The Need to Be Right

Which is more important to you: being right or being happy? When it comes to relationships, the two are often mutually exclusive. If you choose to be right all of the time, you'll create considerable friction in your personal and work relationships. Do you really want to have that argument over something small, just to prove your point, and keep having it every day? As Dr. Phil McGraw would say, "How's that workin' for ya?"

Bliss Key #6: Choose to Be Happy

This is the way of bliss. Every day when you wake up, firmly choose peace, joy, and inner calm. If the events in your life contrive to upset you, bring your attention back to these states of being and use them as a filter. Ask yourself: "Where is the joy in this situation?" or "What belief do I need to let go of in order to achieve true peace?" or "How can my experience of this person's hurtful words increase my sense of inner calm *even more*?"

Bliss Blocker #7: Staying Isolated

Often we think that we're so unique that no one else will be able to understand our life, our world, our problems. Or we're so busy at work that all we can do is come home, eat, and pass out. This is no way to live.

Bliss Key #7: Get Up, Get Out, Get Connected

If life has become a vicious cycle of getting up, going to work, and coming home exhausted, your first priority is to break that cycle. We work-at-homes are often the worst when it comes to this. We hole up in our comfy little home offices with all of our modern conveniences, and suddenly a whole week has gone by with little outside stimulus. Whether you work in an office or at home, if work is your entire universe, your bliss muscle will start to suffocate. Give it air!

If you work at home, schedule time to get out of the house—and stick to it like you would an appointment with your doctor. Establish a regular outing with a friend. If you're in cubicle nation, either plot outings over instant messenger with friendly officemates or investigate nearby social groups that might be happy additions to your life. Many cities have groups that cater to almost every possible desire. You can find them through your local newspaper or at meetup .com. Don't see an interesting meetup near you? Be a pioneer: start a meetup tailored to your tastes. I've been to spinning and weaving meetups, spirituality meetups, biodiesel and eco-awareness meetups, and entrepreneurial meetups of all sorts. Whatever your interests are, there are people out there who share them.

Bliss Blocker #8: Being an Emotio

Memories of less-than-blissful times
ness at the most inconvenient momen
emotional garbage will junk up your (
to connect to your bliss. (The energy
chapters will be a huge help in address
Key will also help in an even simpler wa

Bliss Key #8: Journal Nonblissful Moments Away

In *The Artist's Way* (1992), Julia Cameron introduced the practice
of morning pages: every morning writing down whatever's in your
mind—without prejudice and without pausing to edit, censor, or
delete. Jot everything down—even if it's silly, even if it doesn't follow
standard rules of grammar, even if it makes no sense whatsoever—
and then either archive it or simply delete it. There. Done. Feel better?
Practices like this one can rid the mind of leftover "junk" thoughts
that arrive unbidden into the present and become distracters.

Similarly, journal when faced with frustrating situations. Jot
down everything you can about the particular frustration—without
censoring and without editing. Write until you are finished. When
you're finished, throw your words away. This gets errata out of the
way, clearing your mind for productive thought. Take three deep,
slow breaths. Now is the time to think, journal, or talk about the
problem productively.

Addiction to Negative Input

umb/fat/ugly/I can't get it right …" How much of this
do to yourself? How much of this do you take from others?
en becoming angry when you make mistakes can be destructive.
We also often get negative input from our favorite media sources,
whether that's television, radio, print, or the Internet.

Bliss Key #9: Be Kind to Yourself

While it's important to do the things you have to do, cut yourself
huge breaks. Indulge in a deep belly laugh every day and regulate
your exposure to the media. A decade ago Andrew Weil invited us
in his *Eight Weeks to Optimal Health* (1997), to take a "news fast": to
refrain from watching television, listening to gossip, and reading the
newspaper for an entire week. Give it a try.

Having gossip on the list can be difficult, for that is how women
naturally communicate—most of the time harmlessly. Gossip can
make our social networks strong, but when it turns bad, it can be a
vicious instigator of stress and strife.

Weil and peace activist Norman Cousins are also both propo-
nents of the curative power of laughter. Weil prescribes at least one
deep belly laugh a day. I think that's just great—so I will, too. So pre-
scribed: one good belly laugh, to be taken daily with lots of water.

Bliss Blocker #10: Making Too Much Noise

By living life so "out loud" that you can't hear anyone or anything but yourself, you isolate yourself from the richness of life. Living loudly blocks awareness.

Bliss Key #10: Tread Carefully, Talk Softly

Be mindful of your steps upon the earth. Take stock of how "loud" your presence is—in your home, your neighborhood, your work, and your play. Speaking literally, stop stomping. If you normally run out of the house and fling yourself into your car, experiment with taking each step slowly and deliberately, taking time to enter your car (or public transportation) consciously and carefully. If you normally plop into chairs with a heavy thump, try sitting slowly and with intention, placing your body instead of just letting your muscles go and dropping to the surface below you.

Experiment with *not* speaking when a group is asked a question. Try taking very long pauses to think when you are directly addressed. A hundred years ago, we were encouraged as women to modulate our voices. As a result, from the first years of feminism and onward, many of us raised or deepened our voices artificially to break free of what was considered to be an oppressive political constraint. Allow your voice to come back to its natural pitch and tempo. If you tend to talk over a crowd, soften your voice. It's okay to choose to not be heard for a day or two. Feel what it's like to sit with silence.

Bliss Blocker #11: Being Out of Sync

Do you not have a daily practice that brings you back into centered awareness, either because you're too busy or think meditation is too hard to learn?

Bliss Key #11: Breathe, Meditate, or Simply Be

Meditation is not a competitive sport. It's not complicated, and it doesn't require years of training. To meditate, first let yourself be in the present. Attend to your surroundings, hear the many noises of the world around you, see the interplay of colors and light. If you wish, focus your eyes on a single point in front of you. Focus on something easy to look at so that your eyes naturally feel relaxed. Now turn your attention to your inner self. Clear your mind and just focus on your breath, on the rising and falling of your chest and abdomen. Turning your focus inward, feel the pulsing of your blood as it courses through your veins. Feel the drum of your heartbeat. Feel the breath moving in and out of your body....

If you can keep this up for even just twenty seconds, you'll be meditating. Slowing down and becoming contemplative helps clear stress hormones. If this practice feels good to you, you may also enjoy the contemplation meditation and sage wisdom offered by Buddhist nun Pema Chodron (www.pemachodron.com).

Bliss Blocker #12: Feelings of Entitlement

This is taking what you have and what is given to you for granted; being petulant about deserving more, better, or simply different things than you have; and disdaining gifts because they aren't exactly what you want.

Bliss Key #12: Give Great Gratitude

As we discussed earlier, the Law of Attraction means that when we're connected to gratitude, appreciation, love, and other positive emotions, more of these emotions come into our lives. On the other hand, anger, pain, sadness, and frustration attract more of the same. If you're not presently where you want to be, find things to give thanks for. Spend a few moments feeling love well up in your heart and suffuse your body as you remember the wonderful people, situations, and things in your life. List both all the things that brought you joy today and all the things that drained you. Be grateful for the things that brought you joy, and use the energy therapies you'll learn later in this book to deal with the things that drained, challenged, frustrated, or confused you.

Research by the HeartMath Institute says our heartbeat is "in congruence" when we think about what we are truly grateful for (Childre 1999). Trust your heart. Unlike your tongue, which can say anything, the rest of your body never lies. What is in your heart is the key to getting what you most deeply desire. When in doubt, turn to the emotional guidance system of your body: put your hand over your heart and consider what option is best for you. Remember, your body will never lie to you. What does your heart tell you?

CHAPTER 4

Energy Therapy Quick-Starts for Relaxation, Peace, and Health

*A*s you know by now, the way to bliss lies not in the number of spa visits you can fit into a week, but in a peaceful mind, free of stress and old, troublesome issues. The second part of the Everyday Bliss Process, after you figure out your Bliss List and Shadow List, is to release the old worries, troubles, and issues that sideline both your bliss and a large part of your available energy. The energy therapies you'll learn in the next few chapters are the best ways my clients and I have found to release this kind of stress. Before we sail into the energy therapies themselves,

**This chapter relates to phase 6 of the
Everyday Bliss Process, outlined on page 11.**

however, I'm going to teach you a number of energetic "quick fixes"—and how you can begin working to get your tangled energy back on track right away. Ready? Great! We'll start with a wonderful quick, meridian-based routine to wake you up in the morning and relax you blissfully into sleep.

THE A.M. CLEANSING AND ENLIVENING ROUTINE

This routine may take you a little while to learn, but once you've got it down, it shouldn't take more than ten minutes or so. Its rewards are priceless, well worth your tiny time investment. You can also do one or more of these lovelies during your day to improve your health, beauty, and relaxation even further. Refer to the following acupoint illustration for the points mentioned in the exercises in this chapter.

Upon arising—before leaving the bedroom is best—do the following routine to harmonize and amp up your energy for the day:

1. Shining the Gate of Heaven

   Gather all five fingers of one hand together into a loose fist and place it on the top of your head where a marionette's string would come out, right on the Crown point. Gently scrub the scalp with your fingertips 7 to 10 times in clockwise circles. This opens the crown to receiving a new influx of energy to power your day.

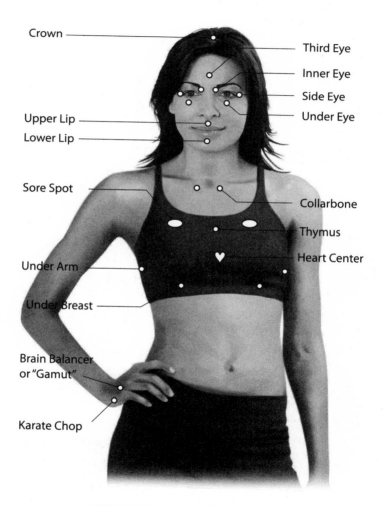

Crown

Third Eye

Inner Eye

Side Eye

Under Eye

Upper Lip

Lower Lip

Sore Spot

Collarbone

Thymus

Heart Center

Under Arm

Under Breast

Brain Balancer or "Gamut"

Karate Chop

THE MERIDIAN ACUPOINTS

2. Forehead Pulls

Interlace the fingers of both hands and place your fingertips to the third eye area of your forehead. (Your little fingers will touch the bridge of your nose and your index fingers your hair; you're using your fingertips to make a line from your nose to your hairline.) Putting pressure on the forehead with your fingertips, pull your hands apart, all the way to the sides of your head. Pull fingertips out to ear level. Do 3 to 5 times to open the third eye chakra for ultimate clarity in your day.

3. The Triple Thump Plus

Vigorously tap your Collarbone points 7 to 10 times, your Thymus point 7 to 10 times, and your Under Breast points 7 to 10 times. This is the traditional "Triple Thump" from *Touch for Health* (Thie 1973) and Educational Kinesiology. Now tap on the Under Arm points 7 to 10 times with gently closed fists. (Remember the chicken dance? This maneuver is similar in position: Gently curl your hands into fists. Bend your elbows to bring your fists to about three inches below where your underarm hair ends. Tap.) Finally, gently rub the "Sore Spot"—the upper chest neurolymphatic drainage point—in a circular motion for a few seconds (don't tap here, it can be very sensitive). This routine is great for general health, wellness, and immune-system armoring. It also helps to fine-tune your body's energy. Do this whole sequence three times in all.

4. A.M. Bilateral Cross Crawl

This exercise hooks up the energy across your body and is a cure for brain fuzz, lack of clarity, and tiredness—all hallmarks of energy not crossing the body correctly. Your body's energy normally exits each of the brain's hemispheres to cross at the neck and then flow down each side of the body. Cross crawling helps coordinate right and left brain hemispheres, improves sight, hearing, general coordination, and spatial awareness. This is a great exercise before a test or big presentation!

THE CROSS CRAWL

Referring to the illustration above, here's how to cross crawl: Stand and touch your left hand to your right knee, lifting the knee up to meet the hand halfway. Then switch, touching your right hand to your left knee. Then touch your left hand to your right knee again, and so on. Advanced users can touch their elbows to their knees. If you're in a wheelchair or bedridden, first cross your ankles and then touch your left hand to your right knee, your right hand to your left knee, and so on. Do this at least 12 times.

5. Homolateral Cross Crawl

   This exercise synchronizes the energy running up and down the left and right sides of your body. Holding onto a chair with your left hand to steady yourself, swing your right arm and leg in unison, back and forth in an easy swinging motion. Do this 10 times. Switch and hold the chair with your right hand and swing your left arm and leg 10 times. Finish this sequence with ten further Bilateral Cross Crawls to seal the correct energy flows into your body.

6. Cook's Hookup

   This is great when you're just frazzled, exhausted, or thinking fuzzily. This exercise hooks up the vibrational energy in your body so that it runs smoothly and infuses you with a sense of calm and relaxation. Refer to the illustration on the opposite page.

COOK'S HOOKUP

Sit with one ankle crossed over the other ankle. Cross one wrist over your other wrist. With your two arms crossed in front, turn your hands over so palms face each other. Clasp the fingers of your crossed hands together.

Bend your elbows outward, bringing your hands closer to your chest, so that your clasped hands naturally rotate under, toward your body (your arms will end up looking rather like a pretzel's center twist—this is called "pretzeling" in Touch for Health circles). Rest your clasped hands against your heart. Breathe gently, in and out, for approximately two minutes.

Next, place feet apart on the floor and uncross your arms. Place your hands together, touching only fingertips to opposite fingertips, hands in a steepled position. Your two thumbs should point toward your heart. Breathe gently for approximately thirty seconds. Release.

7. **Fourfold Breath**

   Breathe in to an easy count of four, hold your breath for a count of four, breathe out for a count of four, and hold for a count of four. Repeat this cycle for at least four minutes. This practice can be especially useful in times of great stress.

8. **Setting Intention for the Day**

   Briefly hold the TAT pose (see TAT pose illustration on page 115) while you clearly set your intention for the day, out loud and in positive terms. The TAT pose hooks you directly into the visual cortex of your brain where all intent is made manifest. Even if you're not a "visualizer," this area of the brain is responsible for attracting that which you desire.

   Hook your daily intention to a personal goal, for example: "Today is about integrity. To practice integrity in my day, I will, as I've promised myself, complete my newsletter before 3 P.M. I will also practice truth-telling with all the people in my life. With love toward all I meet, I will decide when it is best to withhold my thoughts and when it is best to express them."

9. Hydration Throughout the Day

Drink a full glass of water—at least sixteen ounces—before you head out the door. Drinking water throughout the day helps flush toxins that are released from nerves, muscles, organ fibers, and fat, effortlessly out of your body. Drink, and don't be afraid of going to the bathroom—being queen of your own porcelain throne is a luxury. Rejoice in the fact that you're getting cleaner and clearer than you've ever been.

THE P.M. CALMING AND SOOTHING ROUTINE

1. About half an hour before going to bed, do very slow forehead pulls for about a minute to drain any stress hormones down into the lymph system where they can be flushed out. Also, gently rub your Sore Spot a few times on each side in a circular motion.

2. Review your day while holding the TAT pose (see illustration on page 117). Forgive yourself for anything you blame yourself for. It doesn't matter whether you mean it or not; your subconscious mind will get the message to let go. Ditto anything you blame others for.

The TAT pose will allow these and other thought viruses to simply drain away. You'll find yourself quite relaxed after doing the TAT pose—it's also an excellent cure for insomnia!

3. Drink water and allow the last of the day's toxins to filter out so they don't clog your system overnight.

4. Meditate or engage in your favorite before-bed unwinding behavior. Reading in bed and self-massage of the acupoints on the hands and feet are also good ways to unwind both energy snarls and events that linger in your mind.

5. Do the P.M. Cross Crawl: Lying on your back, cross your legs and arms easily at the wrists and ankles. Peacefully breathe in and out 10 times. Relax, and let the cares of the day float away.

6. Enjoy a neurolymphatic release move: Holding the four fingers of each hand together, cup each hand until your fingertips form an even, straight line. Press your fingertips to the sides of your head very, very lightly, about an inch above the outer rim of each ear and slightly toward the back of the head. There is a neurolymphatic point here; holding it drains stress and is deeply relaxing. You'll probably find this tremendously calming. Hold for a minute or so.

7. As the last few minutes to lights-out pass, move your hand to your Heart Center and send yourself love to go to sleep with. Very gently, warm (don't thump!) your thymus with

the other hand. Use your hands to smooth the energy from the top of your head down your body. Part your hands at the groin level and place your palms on the bed. Let any extra energy drain out of your palms.

Make these A.M./P.M. routines part of your everyday life for improved health, mental clarity, and a host of other positive benefits. Once you start to do these two routines daily, you'll be well on your way to bliss.

A FEW EXTRA BLISS-OUT TECHNIQUES

For those times when you just want something to pick you up on the go, here's a first-aid kit at your fingertips!

Brain Fog Remover—Alternated Tapping

You'll learn the primary acupoint tapping therapy, EFT, in the next chapter. Here, however, is a quick practice that contains many (though not all) of the benefits of EFT. Pressing the four main fingers of each hand together so that the fingertips form a single straight line, tap just one inch above the ears. Tap first with the right hand, and then with the left, always alternating your taps. This little maneuver has the effect of synchronizing the right and left hemispheres of the brain and removing brain fog, clumsiness, and stalled thinking. This is great for use as an afternoon pick-me-up.

ALTERNATED TAPPING—PARTNER VARIATION

This is a way to engage someone else's energy system. You can either use it to help heal your own energy or with small children who are too young to tap for themselves. Sit in a comfortable position across from the person you're working with. Keep the image of the thing you most want to achieve from this situation foremost in your mind. Place your hands palm up on your knees; keep them as relaxed as you possibly can. Have your partner use two fingers to tap the centers of your gently opened palms alternately. First right, then left—over and over until you feel done. Shake your hands out and take a deep breath. This practice can also be used to remove negative thoughts or feelings.

Aural Hygiene and the Temporal Tap

This is a bit of a play on words and means keeping your ears clean—energetically speaking. Simultaneously run the tips of your index fingers around the inside rims of your ears; follow these tracks to the insides of the ear and down to the earlobes; give these a gentle tug. Do this three times. Now starting at the front of the ear, place your index finger in the groove where the ear attaches to your head. With slight pressure, run your finger from the front of your ear in this groove, over the top of the ear, and around the back, ending again with a slight tug to the earlobe. Now, reach up and flap the top flexible part of the ear (the pinna) back and forth a few times. Breathe deeply throughout this process. You're actually clearing the energy pathways for the entire body by working with the ear. In acupuncture, the entire body is thought to be represented by various dense, tiny points on the ears; in fact, there's a special branch of acupuncture called auriculotherapy designed specifically to stimulate points in the ear. The next time you have aches and pains— or simply a bad day emotionally—try rubbing your ears like this. It can work wonders!

The "Brain Balancer"

There are vibrational healing points all over the body. Some of these pressure points, like those by the ears, release stress from a number of other areas of the body as well. The "gamut" point on the back of the hand is one of these. In fact, it's a hotline to balancing stress in many different places on the body, most notably the brain.

1. First, find the Gamut point on the acupoint diagram on page 83. It's located between the little-finger and ring-finger bones on the back of the hand. (It exists on both hands; it doesn't matter which you choose to use.) Begin tapping gently on this point with the index finger of your other hand. While you tap on this Gamut point, think of whatever is causing you stress. Tap for thirty seconds.

2. Next, tap on the Crown of your head, right in the center of your skull. This is where all of the acupuncture energy tracks, or meridians, meet up. Tap here for thirty seconds.

3. Return to the Gamut point; tap it for another thirty seconds. Take a huge breath in and then breathe out, releasing all of your stress and tension. Feel the glow of pure, clean relaxation spreading over you.

Now, with your energy revved and ready to go, let's learn the energy therapy techniques that will change your life, your mind, and your state of bliss!

CHAPTER 5

Emotional Freedom Technique: The Active Woman's Friend

$\mathcal{I}$n this chapter you'll learn the first of three energy therapies, all of which you can use to erase the negativity of the past and firmly establish your everyday bliss. These methods have three things in common: they all remove blockages and emotional pain, they all help you create the future you want, and they'll all leave you supremely relaxed and in a state of bliss.

This chapter relates to phase 6 of the Everyday Bliss Process, outlined on page 11.

When you're living a busy, highly scheduled lifestyle, it's important to make time in your schedule for relaxation and stress release. As individuals, we achieve that relaxation response in different ways. Some prefer to release stress through the physical burn of activities like team sports, hiking, or walking. Others prefer more peaceful forms of physical relaxation like massage or yoga. Still others prefer soothing mental practices like rest or meditation. The three energy therapies you'll learn are each geared toward a different level of activity preference. All three methods are equally effective, giving you ample ways to ensure your everyday bliss.

First we'll discuss an energy therapy for women who like to actively pursue their bliss: Emotional Freedom Technique (EFT).

EFT: BACKGROUND AND BASICS

Developed by Gary Craig, Emotional Freedom Technique is an acupoint-tapping routine that releases emotional and physical stress, both instantly and progressively. While tapping gently on acupuncture points is often soothing in the moment, repeated tapping can access and clear deeper and deeper layers of an issue. This releases tension and induces a euphoric sense of peace and well-being that will continue throughout your day.

Until a few years ago, EFT was known only to psychotherapists, performance coaches, and a few lucky members of the lay public who appreciated its swiftness and ease in dissolving blockages. Over the years, EFT has increased in complexity and sophistication, in the process gaining a solid base of master practitioners, advanced and alternative delivery protocols, and adoring fans. Fortunately for bliss-seekers, EFT is both easy to learn and easy to use and astonishingly effective for a variety of issues. I personally used EFT to both end the crushing pain I felt in my broken back and deal with the devastating range of emotions that accompanied my years of recovery.

How EFT Differs from Other Therapies

EFT has racked up some remarkable results, but like all energy therapies, EFT isn't 100 percent effective 100 percent of the time. While EFT isn't a magic bullet, because it is safe, has no reported side effects, and can be easily learned and practiced, it *is* enthusiastically endorsed by noted physicians Norm Shealy and Deepak Chopra for physical and emotional healing.

EFT approaches problems differently than psychotherapy and standard medical science. Like acupuncture, the basic principle of EFT is that "the cause of all negative emotions is a disruption in the body's energy system" (Craig 2006, 17). To correct these imbalances, EFT uses two different therapeutic interventions together:

- A physical program of tapping on sets of powerful acupuncture points to clear negative energy

- A mental program of imagining and reframing stressful incidents to defuse their negative energy

For simplicity's sake, I'll be sharing with you the core method I teach my clients—a fast and simple form of EFT that includes only the best of enhancement protocols. It's quite effective. If you'd like more detailed knowledge about how to work with EFT, nineteen other master practitioners and I have written extensively about the subject in *Freedom at Your Fingertips* (Ball 2006). The information below is more than enough to get you started using EFT, but to augment your effectiveness with more comprehensive techniques, I highly recommend picking up a copy of *Freedom at Your Fingertips* as well.

Basic EFT Procedure

Every time you have a negative experience (like getting yelled at or feeling embarrassed), your body clenches up—and your body's energy streams do too. When an energy stream clenches up, the body's flow of energy becomes blocked. It's like putting a boulder into a river. The river can no longer flow smoothly but must instead flow around the boulder. When a lot of negative things happen in your life, a lot of boulders can end up in your energy stream and, just like a dam on a river, cut you off from a large portion of your body's available energy. This can result in concentration and motivation difficulties and can cause you to replay bad memories over and over again or experience your life as just plain out of sync. Take away these blockages and you'll be able to eliminate the sting of negative emotions, enjoy razor-sharp focus, and glide peacefully through your daily life.

With EFT, you rebalance the body's energy by tapping a sequence of powerful acupoints while holding a negative emotion or situation in mind. This releases the energy that's keeping boulders in your system and allows negative emotions to dissolve. With your balance restored, you can be effortlessly successful, peaceful, and relaxed.

HOW TO ACHIEVE EMOTIONAL FREEDOM WITH EFT

Before beginning to learn EFT, get out your Bliss Journal. As in all your bliss work, take notes to track your progress with EFT over time. List the problem you're focusing on, the date you first begin to work on it, your initial emotional intensity, the phrasing you use, and the date the problem is finally resolved. Also note the phrases you use *after* you finish tapping to test whether the fix is really permanent. (All of this will be further explained below.) Ready to get those boulders out of your energy stream? Let's go.

Step 1: "It's a Setup!"

EFT begins with the Setup, a process to prepare the body and mind for change. If you desperately want to change something but are having a lot of trouble doing so, that's probably because some part of you is getting some benefit from the situation and wants to keep the undesirable memory, emotion, or behavior in place. Usually these reasons aren't consciously known to us. That's okay—we don't have to know what's going on unconsciously to take care of this problem. To get around this part of you that doesn't want to change, simply focus on the problem and do either of the following:

- Form a gentle, loose fist and rub very gently on your Sore Spot in a circular motion. (The Sore Spot is a neurolymphatic conjunction point on the upper chest; see illustration on page 103.)

- Using the side of your hand where the Karate Chop point is located, tap gently on the Karate Chop point of your other hand. By tapping the outer palm sides of the hands together, you send a very powerful clearing pulse through your system.

Either of these processes will work, but choose only one. Next, as you either tap your Karate Chop points or rub continuously on your Sore Spot, say the following Setup Statement three times:

"Even though I have this _____ (fill in the blank with your specific fear, pain, frustration, anxiety, physical symptom, etc.), I deeply and completely accept myself."

Take a deep breath; blow it out. You're done. This process will neutralize any part of you that still wants—for whatever reason—to stay invested in the negative emotion or situation.

Step 2: Rate Your SUDS

SUDS stands for *Subjective Units of Distress*, your measurement of the intensity of the problem or condition you're tapping on. Before you begin the tapping sequence, rate your SUDS on a scale of 0 to 10, with 10 denoting the worst you could possibly feel about the situation and 0 denoting a complete absence of emotional response to the situation. Write this number down: you'll use it later on to evaluate your progress.

Step 3: Identify Your Reminder Phrase

The specific description of your problem that you used in the Setup is also your Reminder Phrase to use while tapping. For example, if your Setup phrase were: "Even though I have this headache, I deeply and completely accept myself," your Reminder Phrase would be "this headache." The more specific your phrase the better, for example, "this anger from the fight I had with my boss" or even "this sadness when I remember how my mother and I never connected before she died."

With EFT, to eliminate the problem at the deepest possible level, it's imperative to be extremely specific about the problem itself and to focus on specific incidents or symptoms or aspects of the problem. Tap on a different aspect of a problem at each point. For example, for a headache you might start with "this headache that pounds like a jackhammer behind my eyes." Then, moving onto a different point, continue "this headache like a spear through the right side of my head," and so on.

Different aspects of a problem can be identified by thinking about what bothers you most about the problem. For example, in a relationship breakup this might include "the way he looked at me when he said goodbye," "the feeling that my heart is dissolving," "how sad I feel every minute of the day," and so on. All of these are aspects. By running through your list of aspects as you tap through the routine, you'll help your body and mind to really zero in on the problem and root it out completely.

Step 4: The EFT Tapping Sequence

To start the EFT sequence, tap 10 times on each of the following acupoints (refer to the illustration on page 103): the Crown, the Third Eye, the Inner Eye, the Side Eye, the Under Eye, the Upper Lip, the Lower Lip, the Collarbone, the Under Arm, and the Under Breast. (On points which lie on both sides of the body, it doesn't matter which side you start with, right or left; however, stick with one side for the first round of tapping; use the points on the other side during the next round of tapping.)

At each point, as you tap you'll repeat one of the Reminder Phrases you discovered. The following is an example of a round of EFT using phrases someone might typically use for headache pain:

1. Tapping the Crown or top of the head (where a marionette's string would be attached) 10 times, saying, "this headache"

2. Tapping the forehead on the Third Eye, saying, "this hammering inside my head"

3. Tapping the Inner Eye (where the eyebrow starts, at the bridge of the nose), saying, "this pain that radiates down my neck"

4. Tapping the Side Eye (the bony socket where the eye points toward the ear), saying, "the way bright light really hurts when my head is pounding"

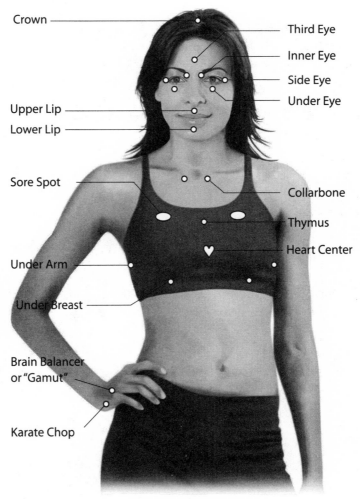

THE EFT TAPPING POINTS

5. Tapping the Under Eye (the "eye bag" area, tapping not on the eyeball but on the bony socket), saying, "this feeling like my head's splitting open"

6. Tapping the Upper Lip, saying "this damned headache"

7. Tapping the Lower Lip, saying "this headache that I can't afford to have because I need to get work done"

8. Tapping under the Collarbone (under the "corner" of the t-junction of the collarbone and the sternum), saying, "this doggone headache!"

9. Tapping the Under Arm point (about three inches below where the armpit hair ends), saying, "this feeling of being tired and overwhelmed by the pounding in my head"

10. Tapping the Under Breast point (in the middle of the first rib under the crease of the breast, directly under the nipple), saying, "this headache that's like a hammer right on my forehead"

Step 5: Taking a Break

Breathe in deeply and fully, exhaling any residual negative energy. Having now completed one set of tapping, take your SUDS rating again to see where you are. Many times a problem will have disappeared after just this simple correction.

Most of the time, though, some of the problem will remain, and you'll need to continue tapping. When this happens, do a second set of tapping on the points above. As you tap this second set, say, "this *remaining* headache," "this *remaining* hammering in my head," and so on. Two such sets constitute one round of EFT. Take your SUDS rating after each completed set. Enjoy watching your intensity dwindle to zero.

If you're not seeing relief in twenty minutes, record your results and come back to the issue in a few days. It may be that you need time to rest and integrate the results of your EFT work; you may also want to address the issue with one of the other energy therapies you learn in this book. For stubborn issues, changes in perspective or the use of new tools can turn the tide. Most issues clear relatively swiftly with consistent practice of EFT.

TAIL-ENDERS TO WATCH FOR

While you're tapping, you may encounter thoughts, memories, or scenes that are outside the focus of what you're tapping on. For example, tapping on your father yelling at you might remind you of a time your teacher or mother yelled at you. This is called a *tail-ender* and often is another aspect of the same problem. Write these tail-enders down—they're further issues to tap on—but stay focused on the emotion or incident you're already tapping on. Once this incident is cleared, then you can start tapping on tail-enders.

Speed EFT

To erase negative emotions even faster, first tap as normal, ten taps at each point going *down* the body from the Crown to the Under Arm point. Then, without taking a break or reassessing SUDS, tap from the Under Arm point back *up* the body to the Crown. Quickly go up and down, several times, until you either feel the need to take a deep breath, sigh, stretch, or feel your energy shifting in some other way. Take your SUDS again and note how your emotions or symptoms have changed. Speed EFT is great for helping you to deeply relax when stressed or when having difficulty falling asleep.

Slow EFT

There are many benefits to tapping *very* slowly, with even more taps—20 or more times on each point—breathing gently and deeply as you release. Slower tapping goes much deeper, addressing more of the roots of the problems you're working on.

There's a time for fast EFT and a time for slow. Your body will let you know which you need. Experiment with both and have fun!

Getting Specific

You'll only get amazing results with EFT when you take the time to be excruciatingly specific about your problem. I can't emphasize enough how important this is. Consider problems as balls of tangled threads. In order to untangle these threads, you have to take each thread by its end and work it out, then tackle the next one, and so on. Eventually, you reach a point where the whole ball falls apart. When you're using EFT to work on a problem, tap on the problem's specific individual threads, not the whole big, hairy, tangled mess. After tapping on several individual threads of the problem, you may find that the whole big, hairy mess then simply falls apart.

The more specific you can be, the better able your mind will be to focus on the exact aspect to transform or eliminate. In your practice of EFT, be diligent in unraveling a problem's individual threads—and be persistent!

GOING TO THE MOVIES: EFT STYLE

Having a framework or context in which to deal with specific incidents can make EFT even easier. I like to use a framework I call "Going to the Movies." For example, say you want to eliminate the negative emotional charge of an incident in which your father yelled at you. His yelling may not have been the only part of the incident that laid down a negative emotional charge within you. By reviewing this incident as a movie, you can experience the scene from several different angles—and thus eliminate myriad different emotions.

Give the movie of your problem a name and write it in your Bliss Journal. Let's call this movie *Dad Yelled at Me for Wrecking the Car.* Next, see the scene unfold in front of you: First, your father comes into the room with an angry look on his face. From your experience of him as an angry man, you know what's coming. Your body starts to clench up and your endocrine glands begin to manufacture stress hormones. Count this as tapping incident #1 and give it a title: "Dad looked angry, and my whole body clenched up." Give it a SUDS rating and use regular rounds of EFT to tap it down to zero. Next, your father may have crossed the room and grabbed you by the arm, frightening you. See this happening and count this as tapping incident #2: "Dad grabbed my arm real hard." Rate it separately and tap it to zero. The actual yelling would then be tapping incident #3; see it playing out just like a movie in front of you and tap it to zero. After being yelled at, you may have experienced a negative reaction—guilt, shame, anger, and so on—this would be tapping incident #4; see, feel, and tap it down as well. Having tapped all four of these incidents away, ask yourself: Is there anything left? If so, dialogue with yourself about what you're feeling as you tap that down, too.

Remember to take a deep breath after each tapping cycle. This will help move the energy up and out of the tangled mess of the issue. I like taking three deep breaths, blowing them out fully and really enjoying the relaxation at the end of the session.

Using this movie framework can greatly increase your chances of getting completely, permanently free of what's bothering you.

FROM LITTLE TO NONE: GETTING RID OF THAT LAST LITTLE BIT OF TENSION

When the SUDS, or emotional intensity, that you feel about a tapping issue is at a 1 on the 0 to 10 scale—or almost completely gone—an eye roll can often take away the remaining intensity without the need to resort to another round of EFT. We explored the infinity eye roll in chapter 4. For some people this isn't comfortable and can make them a bit dizzy. If you find that happening, do an eye asterisk instead.

Using the asterisk below, hold your head in a stable position and take your eyes up the vertical line of the asterisk to the ceiling, and then down to the floor, four times, up and down, up and down. Next trace the horizontal line of the asterisk all the way to the right of your vision and then to the left, four times. Finally, trace each of the diagonal lines similarly up and then down, four times. Coming back to center, allow the eyes to rest naturally. Take a deep, cleansing breath.

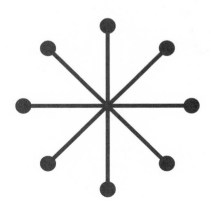

Allow your eye travel to take no more than fifteen seconds and keep your head facing straight forward. Before you begin the asterisk pattern, say your Reminder Phrase just once. Upon completion, take a big, deep breath and rate your SUDS again. Repeat until you no longer experience any negative feelings about the problem at all.

This is a great time to take notes in your Bliss Journal. The more you write things down, the more you'll be able to recognize the patterns of force and power in your life. Also, as you clear unwanted memories and negative incidents, you'll see new patterns—positive, supportive, and life-affirming patterns—begin to emerge.

Starting with your Shadow List that you made in chapter 1, write down every upsetting event you can remember. Go as far back as you can. Some of these events will be from childhood. Don't be surprised if you have fifty, a hundred, or even a couple of hundred. Most people do; this is normal. Start to work on these memories, one by one. Be slow but thorough—there's no need to hurry, you have all the time in the world.

In chapter 9 you'll learn the Personal Peace Process; this will help you get rid of all of the negative feelings that are preventing you from having a peaceful mind and heart. It's powerful and begins now, as you make your all-inclusive Shadow List. Note your progress in your Bliss Journal and keep going!

A Bonus for You

Sometimes it helps to see it in person. Come and see the special video of the EFT Tapping Sequence I've prepared for you at www.every daybliss.org. When you register—and this is free—the EFT video will be one of the many items instantly available to you.

CHAPTER 6

Tapas Acupressure Technique:
Gentle Relief for a Woman's Soul

apas Acupressure Technique, or TAT, was created by Tapas Fleming (1999), a licensed acupuncturist in Southern California. Like EFT, TAT is a meridian therapy. The gentlest form of meridian energy therapy I have found, TAT is the ideal technique for those who prefer a calmer path to clearing stress and achieving bliss. TAT involves lightly holding a few acupressure points on your head while you run through a series of mental shifts. The particular acupoints used connect to the visual cortex of your brain, the center of visualization. The combination

**This chapter relates to phase 6 of the
Everyday Bliss Process, outlined on page 11.**

of this hotline to your brain and your deep focus on an issue can free you of discomfort and unblock your energy, opening the way to bliss.

Tapas is a Sanskrit term denoting a focused effort toward bodily purification and spiritual enlightenment. Because the acupoints used can sometimes stimulate a mild sensation of warmth as your body's energy shifts and your perceptions change, it is suggested that you hold the TAT acupoints no more than twenty minutes a day, rest briefly afterward, and—as with all energy therapies—drink plenty of water. (Note that this twenty-minute limit doesn't refer to time spent on the entire clearing process, just the time you spend actually holding TAT acupoints.)

WHY USE TAT?

TAT, EFT, and the upcoming ZPoint Process all work superbly well; each has its fans. For women who like to be active, the tapping routine of EFT is often the favorite. Those who prefer calm, meditative, body-centered transformations tend to love TAT. You can use the steps of TAT to address everything from the minor frustrations of a bad day to deep issues—or to set a firm intention to create a blissful future. Parents can also use TAT on babies and children when EFT tapping might wake a sleeping baby or agitate a fretful child.

You can use TAT just as effectively as EFT to clear all the old problems that linger in your life. You can also use TAT to leave the fast track and plug yourself back into your bliss whenever you notice a problem that takes you out of peaceful balance. I suggest using TAT as the energy therapy component of the Personal Peace Process you'll learn in chapter

9. Try it—when you do, you'll be amazed at the energy, enlightenment, and peace that fills and elevates your life.

TAT and Bliss

Many of my clients love to use TAT to dissolve personal traumas, as it feels, to quote one of them, "like my muscles have melted, just like a good massage," or, as another said, like "snuggling all warm and cozy in my favorite blanket." The more personal issues you clear with TAT, the more tension dissolves—and the more relaxation has the chance to rush in. Take some time after each TAT session to enjoy the delicious soothing feeling it produces in both your body and your mind. Each TAT session will reinforce this sense of bliss; every time you hold the TAT pose and run through the steps, your bliss will deepen further. Once you memorize the steps of TAT, it won't take you more than five minutes to complete a full TAT session. Below is the way I personally perform TAT. A few steps are shortened versions of the original format; my clients and I have found these as effective as the original steps, but these take less time.

THE STEPS OF TAT

The Dedication: Before starting any TAT session affirm: "I dedicate this work for the benefit of all of my ancestors, all of my family, all parts of me and all points of view I have ever had, and anyone else who might gain benefit from it."

115

When we dedicate our TAT practice this way, entire families sometimes receive healing in unexpected ways: relationships may mend, old hurts may suddenly evaporate, or physical healing may begin.

After dedicating your session, place your hands gently in the position seen in the picture on the opposite page. This is the TAT Pose; here's how you to do it.

Place the thumb and ring finger of one hand (either hand will do) on your Inner Eye points (refer to the acupoint diagram on page 103), roughly one-eighth of an inch above the inner point of the eye. Rest your middle finger lightly on your Forehead point, where your "third eye" is located. Your index and little fingers can rest on the face, curl up against your palm, or just hang out wherever they feel best—where these fingers are placed doesn't matter. With your other hand, cover the back of your head and let your thumb rest on the lower skull line, as if you were cradling your head while doing a sit-up.

If the finger positioning of the front hand is difficult for you, you can do one of two things:

- Cover your eye points with your thumb and middle finger, and your third eye with your index finger.

- Cover your eyebrows and forehead with your hand. Although stimulating the actual points is more effective, a flat hand will cover all the points concerned and work almost as well. This is also the position you'd use if you were doing TAT on a small child whose facial features were too small for adult fingers to comfortably cover the points involved.

116

THE TAT POSE

Step 1

With your hands in the TAT pose, place your mind on the problem and say to yourself, "Everything that led up to _____ happened, it's over, and I'm okay now." You can either name the problem directly or, if you prefer, just use "this" in your phrasing.

Here's an example: "Everything that led up to my being passed over for the promotion I know I deserved happened, it's over, and I'm okay now."

If the problem is ongoing, say, "is happening, and I'm okay" instead.

When you finish a step, take a slight break from the TAT pose—a few seconds will do. Then resume the pose and proceed to the next step.

Step 2

While in the TAT pose say, "Thank you for healing all the places in my mind, body, and life where this has been stored, and healing the deepest origins of this problem."

Keep your hands in the TAT pose for thirty seconds to a minute, or until you feel done with this step. Then let your hands gently fall into your lap. Take a deep breath to help lift the energy of this problem out of the deep recesses where it has been lodged.

Who are you thanking and why? These are good questions. Gratitude for your life, present circumstances, and transformations is not only important, it is *imperative* to your healing. Address your gratitude either to your own personal concept of a higher power or simply the universe in general.

This attitude of gratitude is the first of a triad of powerful attractor factors built into the TAT process. As mentioned earlier, gratitude can be a powerful catalyst for the subconscious mind to move the forces of the universe to begin rearranging your world for you

Step 3

While in the TAT pose say, "I apologize to everyone I have hurt related to this, including myself. I wish us all love, happiness, and peace."

Again, hold the TAT pose until you feel done, and then let your hands drop. Inhale a deep breath. Feel peace flow into you as you allow your body to release.

Sincerely regretting and apologizing for any potentially hurtful actions (even if you don't consciously think you've done anything wrong) is the second powerful attractor in the TAT triad. Sincere apology opens you to healing and lets previously blocked energy flow back into your life.

Step 4

While in the TAT pose say, "I forgive everyone who hurt me or that I blamed related to this, including myself. I wish us all love, happiness, and peace."

Forgiveness—of others and yourself—is the third powerful attractor in the TAT triad. Unconditionally forgiving people, yourself, and your concept of a higher power opens a nice clean space in your personal energy field to receive the healing you are requesting. Take your time with this one; let your hands stay in the pose as long as you need. When you're ready, let your hands fall, and take a deep breath to move the energy along.

Step 5

While in the TAT pose say, "All the parts of me that got some benefit from this are healing."

Keep your hands in place for thirty seconds, or until you feel done, and then take another deep breath. Notice how relaxed you feel and what a relief it is to take each deep breath.

No matter how unwanted a behavior might be, some part of you—perhaps just a wee tiny part—gets some positive benefit from it. Happily, you don't have to know what that benefit is to dissolve it with this step.

Step 6

With your hands in the TAT pose, say, "Whatever is left about this is healing now."

Keep your hands in place until you feel done with this step, then let them fall. Take another deep breath.

Step 7

With your hands again in the TAT pose, say, "I choose _____" (whatever it is that you want instead of the problem). Again, stay in the pose for thirty seconds or until you feel done. Then drop your hands and take a deep, cleansing breath. What you have just chosen is already rushing toward you.

Fully flesh out your choice. See it, hear it, smell it, feel it deep in your body. The more vividly you can experience and articulate your choice, the better for complete transformation, for example, "My boss and I get along great. She constantly promotes me to others and helps me gain more skills and connections. She always keeps me abreast of changes in the department and is cheerful and positive whenever we interact."

Step 8

With your hands in the TAT pose, say, "Thank you for completely integrating this healing now."

Again, address your thanks to either your own concept of a higher power or the universe in general. Hold this last step until you feel done. Feel relaxation wash over you.

Take a final deep breath—you've now finished a round of TAT. Once you become proficient in it, the whole process need only take a few minutes.

PRACTICE NOTES AND MECHANICS

If you've never done TAT before, you may first need to clear some basic assumptions that can cause TAT not to work. With your hands in the TAT pose, spend a few moments concentrating on each of the following three statements:

- "TAT is too easy to work or be of any value."

- "TAT is easy and could work and be of great value."

- "I deserve to live and I accept love, help, and healing."

You're now ready to use the TAT process on any problem you like!

TAT will deeply relax you; as a result, sometimes you may find your hands slipping out of position. If this happens or if your arms tire easily, lie on your bed and prop both arms up with pillows. TAT, like EFT, has the tendency to leave you so relaxed that at times you may feel that you need a nap or a break. Be sure to allow some time at the end of each of your TAT practices for a natural short rest.

As with EFT, a single round of TAT may not be enough to dissolve your issue. If you feel an issue needs further resolution, go through the steps of TAT again. Several repetitions may be needed. This is okay. Respect the clues that your body and mind give you. You're on a journey—enjoy the ride; you'll know when you've arrived.

TAT for Relationships

The amount of energy we waste each day in keeping old grudges, hurts, and disappointments alive is phenomenal. Healing relationships that tug at you with grief, sadness, or anger is very important to regaining a sense of everyday bliss. When you clear and release old, stuck energy through TAT or any of the other energy therapies, not only will you feel immediately lighter, more energized, and at peace, you'll also find that the problematic relationships start to heal—sometimes even healing completely overnight.

People who have cleared relationship woes using TAT often report hearing from the person in the relationship they were working on the following day. Old friends and estranged family members suddenly call out of the blue, and a beautiful new future becomes possible. While this may or may not happen, by working through relationship difficulties, you'll free yourself from the accompanying burden of old guilt, anger, and sorrow.

Whether your relationship difficulty is with someone living or dead, you can address the problem by holding the TAT pose and either running through the steps or having a candid, honest conversation with the person in your mind. If, during this imaginary conversation, the person replies to things you tell them, listen with sincerity. It's amazing how often the things you "hear" in personal energywork sessions parallel—often exactly—the things the other party will tell you in person when you make contact with them in real life.

Save a portion of this conversation to thank the other person for all the wonderful lessons you learned from them and to forgive them for anything you've been holding against them. Consciously release anything you may still be holding against the other person by holding the

TAT pose and intending the release to happen. Once you have forgiven the other person, ask for forgiveness from them for anything you may have done to them during the course of your relationship—even if you think you've behaved well. This step will open up huge flows of positive energy and peaceful feelings in your life.

Intimately Personal: Self-Work with TAT

When working on relationships, don't forget the most important one—your relationship with yourself. Use TAT to forgive yourself for not meeting your own expectations, for "failing," for being inattentive, for messing up, for being just plain human. Revisit all of the incidents that you can remember where you've hit yourself in the middle of the head in anger over your own perceived incompetence, and this time, allow the healing waves of forgiveness and release to wash over you as you hold the TAT pose. As with all of your energy work, note the incidents you worked on, as well as your progress, in your Bliss Journal.

TAT encourages us to be especially kind with ourselves, to laugh at our mistakes and to readily forgive them with love in our hearts. Allow love for self to permeate your entire being each and every time you hold the TAT position. Reflect on how precious a gift to the world you are, and how dear and funny and wonderful a thing life is as it manifests through you.

SUMMONING SELF-LOVE

People often have difficulty loving themselves. This exercise can help you if you find working on your relationship with yourself difficult. I didn't love myself very much when I started using energy therapies. I was in a bad marriage, immobilized in bed with an excruciatingly painful broken back, and had an attitude full of bent nails and broken glass. But I had the blessings of a mother who loved me unreservedly and a cat I adored, both of whom taught me a thing or two about how to love. I have only to visualize my mom or kitty's face to feel myself softening and opening up, to myself and others.

If you have a hard time mustering up much love for yourself, think of someone whom you love unreservedly. Puppies, kittens, or other pets can jumpstart us here, as we tend to have pure love for our animal friends, without any complex attachments. Children or significant others can also be good subjects to focus on. Think of the object of your love until you get an "Awwww! What a sweet little darling!" feeling.

Now, let this feeling of unconditional love flow into your hands, like a warm ball of energy. Feel and see it pulsing there, sweet and beautiful, warm and glowing. You may see a color or colors in this ball of energy, or it may be clear. Whatever it feels and looks like will be right for you.

Feel this ball of loving energy growing heavier and heavier. When the time feels right, affirm: "I choose to love myself" and bring the hand holding the energy ball up to your chest and put the whole ball of energy into your heart. Feel yourself begin to float as your heart becomes lighter and lighter with the love you now have for yourself.

FURTHER WORK IN TAT

While the descriptions above are the core techniques of TAT as a healing process, you may come across some situations that require in-depth training, skill, and expertise. If you meet with resistance—or things just aren't working—remember that there is no failure, only feedback. Consider consulting a professional. Always be sure to document your progress; your Bliss Journal can be invaluable in helping you figure out—on your own or with the help of a therapist or an energy coach—how to shift what isn't working. Like EFT, TAT is a therapy where persistence and repeated clearings provide the most comprehensive healing and release.

CHAPTER 7

ZPoint Process—Energy
Therapy on the Go!

$\mathcal{N}$ow, you may be thinking, "I'm just an ordinary Jane. I don't know if I can learn all these acupoints. What if I can't touch the points—or don't want to—or have my hands full? Can energy therapy still work for me?" Of course it can! ZPoint Process, the third of our powerful energy therapies, is a great technique for those who want to clear issues and attain bliss completely through the power of their minds. If you've ever been speeding down the highway, mad as heck because someone

**This chapter relates to phase 6 of the
Everyday Bliss Process, outlined on page 11.**

cut you off, you're going to love this one—you can do it while driving, putting on your shoes, or typing on the computer. It's the energy therapy for those of us who feel we "can't take the time" and are always on the go. With ZPoint Process there's no longer any excuse—this energy therapy practically runs itself!

ZPoint Process was developed by Canadian hypnotherapist Grant Connolly (2006). Alone of the energy therapies presented in this book, ZPoint Process relies only upon the powerful energy of your mind: the energy of intention. This is an elegant therapy you simply concentrate on for profound relief—no meridians, no acupoints. ZPoint can be practiced invisibly in the boardroom, classroom, and especially in that "counting to ten" space when dealing with parenting or relationship frustrations. I even use ZPoint while driving to take away the tension of rush hour. ZPoint gives you an effortless, effective way to take control of your life and your reactions to it.

HOW ZPOINT WORKS

ZPoint features a short healing program that you'll read to your subconscious mind—only the one time, ever. Your subconscious is the part of you actually doing the work in ZPoint—it is a faithful friend and helper that listens to everything you say to yourself. It will be listening when you read the following program and also when you ask it to help you in the future. The subconscious loves to help out—that's the job it does best! To transform it into a powerful ally that will help you get what you want, all you need to do is provide it with a bit of structure. After you've read the healing program to yourself, all you'll need to do in the future to achieve relaxation and bliss is activate the cue word of your choice.

After using ZPoint for a while, many people experience a dramatic, immediate, and long-lasting reduction in their overall levels of stress. They report enjoying clearer, quieter, and more focused minds. Many notice improvements in relationships with coworkers, bosses, friends, family members, and even strangers.

As an added perk, many people feel as though they enter a deep meditative state while practicing ZPoint. Imagine feeling relaxed, peaceful, and filled with the most delicious sense of well-being without hours of chanting or the intense focus required by a formal meditation. When you practice ZPoint, that's how you'll feel in moments.

Choosing Your Cue Word

First, you need to choose a cue word. This should be a word you can say quickly and repetitively, without stumbling. You'll insert this word into the healing program below. After you program this cue word into your subconscious, change will be triggered by saying this cue word over and over, either aloud or in your mind. Every time you repeat your cue word as you focus on areas of stress, you'll release stress and begin to feel better.

Choose something positive for your cue word. Avoid words with double or possibly negative meanings, like "power", "sex" or "money." Successful cue words others have chosen include "bliss," "love," "peace," "harmony," "breathe," "yes," "now," "om," "amen," "happy," and so on.

Whatever works for you, in whatever language you're comfortable with, will be just fine.

Although the healing program, once read, is yours for life, you're not stuck with just one cue word. If you want, you can have more than one. Just tell your subconscious, "We're also using _____ (fill in the additional cue word) as a cue word now." If you want to decommission a certain cue word, just tell your subconscious mind, "_____ (name the cue word you're decommissioning) is no longer my cue word. My cue word is now _____." Presto! It's done.

You can also develop different cue words for different applications in your life. One of my clients, Sophie, is a rabid soccer fan. Her favorite English team, Manchester United—or "Man-U"—reminds her of strength, vision, and glory. "Man-U" is the perfect cue for her business goals. Sophie's ideal for having it all together in her personal life is Maya Angelou, and so "Maya" is Sophie's cue for dealing with personal issues. A young woman I mentored lost her beloved dog, Breezy. Since Breezy represented all things good to her, "Breezy" became her cue word. If you use someone's name as a cue, take care that all of your associations with that name are positive.

Now, got your cue word? Good. Simply read the statement below to yourself—silently or aloud—and say your cue word when you come to the blank. Read the whole thing once, and your cue word and healing program will be installed for life. Easy! (**Note:** the healing program below includes a reference to a technique known as the *Erase-the-Tape technique*. This will be explained later in the chapter.)

The ZPoint Process Healing Program

Read the following to yourself once, inserting the cue word you've chosen in the blank provided:

> *I hereby set a powerful intention, within you, my sub-conscious mind, to effect the best of all possible outcomes by this clearing, and that each time I notice a pattern or patterns I wish to eliminate, as I say or think my cue word: _____ , you will eliminate all such patterns and components of patterns completely and safely, and each time I repeat my cue word in sequence, you will access deeper and deeper layers and all parts and all aspects of my being.*
>
> *I hereby set a powerful intention, that each time I use the Erase-the-Tape technique, I release all thoughts, memories, beliefs, attitudes, emotions, assumptions, decisions, agreements, and conclusions I've ever experienced concerning whatever emotion, thought, or circumstance that I direct my attention toward, and I represent 10 as this moment in time or any time I choose, and 0 as the first time ever, any of these issues became a problem, and you, my sub-conscious mind, will erase the tape on everything in between. (Connolly 2006, 20-21)*

That's it: your cue word is now installed, and you can begin doing ZPoint clearings. You never have to refer to this installation program again.

THE STEPS OF A BASIC ZPOINT CLEARING

The ZPoint Process itself is quite simple: Focus on an area where you're experiencing stress or feeling distinctly unblissful and say the statements below aloud or to yourself. After you say each of these clearing statements, simply repeat your cue word over and over for fifteen seconds. Repeat your cue until you experience a shift. This could be a sense of your muscles loosening, your tongue or neck relaxing, or a calmer mental feeling. This usually occurs within fifteen to thirty seconds.

Using this process, you can clear negative feelings, patterned behaviors (those endless loops that kick off in response to certain situations), the reasons behind these behaviors (which we don't need to know), and the emotions that drive these reasons and patterns. Test drive your brand new cue word using the Basic ZPoint Protocol:

Step 1: "I clear all of the ways that I feel _____ ." (Fill in the blank with your feeling or problem.) Repeat your cue word ten to fifteen times.

Step 2: "I clear all of the patterns connected to all of these ways." Repeat your cue word ten to fifteen times.

Step 3: "I clear all of the reasons connected to all of these ways." Repeat your cue word ten to fifteen times.

Step 4: "I clear all of the ways these patterns and reasons are held in my body." Repeat your cue word ten to fifteen times.

Step 5: "I clear all of the emotions connected to all of these patterns." Repeat your cue word ten to fifteen times. (Connolly 2006, 22)

Now that you have had a chance to try a ZPoint clearing for yourself, let's take a closer look at what we do in each step.

In step 1, we affirm, "I clear all of the ways...." Using this statement, you literally clear all of the possible ways you feel a single emotion or group of emotions linked to a problem. In ZPoint, unlike in TAT or EFT, you do not have to articulate how you're experiencing negative emotions, nor do you have to be able to identify all of the individual emotions. With ZPoint, you work from the general to the specific so that the results generalize into as many areas as possible. Often it will be enough to just place your awareness on an area of discomfort and release it using this statement.

In step 2, we affirm, "I clear all of the patterns...." Patterns are mindless repetitions of the same behaviors over and over again that are activated and managed by emotional triggers in our lives. An example of a pattern behavior is the sequence of trancelike actions you perform when you brush your teeth or take a shower. You don't need to consciously make sure you've washed every bit of your body or brushed every tooth—you've done it so many times before, you've created a pattern that your mind follows by rote.

Keying into a patterned behavior is like pressing play on a CD: an emotional trigger presses a button inside of you, and off goes the pattern. Much of our day-to-day behavior is patterned response. This can be useful, like tooth brushing, or harmful, like panic attacks, compulsive addictions, or mental tapes that play over and over, making you feel bad about yourself. Clearing all the patterns attached to a problem makes sure these harmful patterns are eliminated. This step releases great amounts of energy for more healthy uses.

In step 3, we "clear all the reasons..." as there may be many reasons we're not consciously aware of. Not qualifying exactly what "reasons" allows all possible reasons to be effectively addressed.

In step 4, clearing all the ways a problem is held in the body allows even often puzzling physical symptoms, tendencies, and neuro-muscular tension to release. If you are dealing with physically manifested stress, this step will help you to move past it.

In step 5, we affirm, "I clear all of the emotions..." As we know from the Law of Attraction, our emotions are a guidance system that can steer us toward success or failure. They can also lock patterns of behavior into place. When you clear the emotions from a pattern, that pattern no longer has the power to control you. As noted above, in ZPoint you don't have to know what emotions are being cleared. By making this affirmation, the emotions that keep you blocked, locked, and immovable are swept away, releasing the energy previously bound up in the pattern behaviors. This released energy can now attract those things you most deeply desire.

Linking

For deeper and more comprehensive clearings, when you can identify the emotions you're experiencing, you can *link* your "I clear all the ways" statements. Linking is simply clearing a number of related emotions, one after another, and then ending the sequence with the final two steps of the Basic ZPoint Protocol. I particularly like to use linking for road rage and waiting in lines. It works! Here are some examples:

- "I clear all of the ways that I am stressed." (Repeat your cue word ten to fifteen times as usual.)

- "I clear all of the ways that driving in traffic causes me to be stressed." (Cue.)

- "I clear all of the ways that I am impatient with the slow guy in front of me." (Cue.)

- "I clear all of the ways that I hate being stuck in traffic." (Cue.)

- "I clear all of the ways that I'm starting to panic that I might be late." (Cue.)

- "I clear all of the ways that all of these issues have been held in my body." (Cue.)

- "I clear all of the ways that all of these issues have been held in my energy field." (Cue.)

- "I clear all of the patterns connected to all of these ways." (Cue.)

- "I clear all of the emotions connected to all of these patterns." (Cue.)

The Fill-in-the-Blank Method

This method is particularly helpful when you don't know where the trouble lies but want to address the issue at its deepest levels. By leaving a blank at the end of your sentence before repeating your cue word, you'll allow your deep mind to select the reason or reasons most important to clear. Simply bring the problem to mind and then use the ZPoint clearing statements, allowing the subconscious mind to "fill in" whatever is necessary.

For example, use procrastination as the problem to be cleared and "bliss" as the cue word:

- "I clear all the ways I procrastinate on finishing my project because _____.... Bliss bliss bliss bliss bliss bliss bliss bliss bliss bliss bliss bliss bliss bliss bliss."

- "I clear all the ways I procrastinate on finishing my project when _____.... Bliss bliss bliss bliss bliss bliss bliss bliss bliss bliss bliss bliss bliss bliss bliss bliss."

- "I clear all the ways I procrastinate on finishing my project whenever _____.... Bliss bliss bliss bliss bliss bliss bliss bliss bliss bliss bliss bliss bliss bliss bliss."

- "I clear all the ways I procrastinate on finishing my project but _____.... Bliss bliss bliss bliss bliss bliss bliss bliss bliss bliss bliss bliss bliss bliss bliss."

And so on. Proceed to clear all of the patterns, reasons, and ways the issue is held in the body and the emotions, just as in the regular ZPoint clearing method.

If you notice yourself yawning, stretching, or even feeling a little bit sleepy, that's good! Your body/mind is releasing the energy that was bound up in keeping these "ways" that this issue was held inside of you. Enjoy the relaxation!

THE OPENING STATEMENT

You can use ZPoint even when you're "in the moment" of a particularly stressful situation. Think about what you're going through and say, "When I think about _____ (fill in the blank with what you're dealing with), I feel _____ (fill in the blank with what you're feeling that you don't want to)." Repeat your cue word either 10 to 15 times or until you feel done, for example, "When I think about the way my kids fight I feel frustrated" or "When I think about the presentation I have to make this Wednesday I feel very nervous." Using just this single statement can clear tremendous amounts of stress; still, ideally you should follow it with the rest of the ZPoint clearing statements, as described above.

THE ZPOINT ERASE-THE-TAPE TECHNIQUE

Remember the old cassette tapes that stored audio and data in the pre-digital era? Lots of us play old information on similar endless-loop tapes inside our minds and bodies. These can affect us very negatively. With cassette tapes, passing a strong magnet over them would erase their contents. Erased tapes would become completely blank and could then have new information recorded onto them. We can similarly use the ZPoint Process to erase the internal "tapes" of stored mental and physical information that we no longer want or need. And we can use that energy previously bound up in these tapes to create another state that we do want—a healthier, more relaxed, peaceful state.

The Erase-the-Tape technique relies heavily on the power of intention and thought to effect change in the subconscious mind. With Erase the Tape (ETT), you can release every thought, memory, belief, attitude, emotion, assumption, and conclusion that does not serve you well. The nice part is that this technique lifts you out of the situation, out of time and space, and directly into the heart of the problem to deal with it safely and securely.

To do this, you'll focus briefly on your problem and then count backward from 10 to 0, with 10 representing the present time and 0 representing the moment of your conception or the first time that the issue first started to be a problem for you; after each count you'll repeat your cue word. Your powerful subconscious mind will then "erase the tape" on everything in between that relates to the issue you're focusing on. Just as in EFT and TAT, you'll remember what happened, but it won't have the negative hold over you it once did. Here's how it works.

Step 1: Identify the Area You Want to Focus On

This could be a relationship, a health condition, an unwanted belief, an addiction, a fight with your boss or partner, negative self-talk, or some other issue. There are no limitations on what you can erase. Open your mind to allow yourself the widest range of possibilities for creating wellness and inner peace with this technique. Erase the Tape on anything that upsets, disturbs, or imbalances you.

On a sheet of paper, draw a large circle. Write the topic of this ETT session in the center of the circle and then write every limiting thought, memory, belief, attitude, emotion, assumption, and conclusion that comes to mind inside the circle, too. This bundles up the various components that go into your issue, which will help you eliminate the negative patterns linked to this topic.

Draw or simply imagine a big red ribbon tied around your bundle, in the center of its containment circle. Give the bundle a name— describe the situation and write that description on the bundle, within its circle. This name can be very simple, like the movie titles we spoke of in chapter 5. For example, if you're working on your relationship with your children, you might have a bundle named: *I Snapped at Little Joey and Made Him Cry—I'm a Bad Mother!*

Step 2: Set Your Intention

You've already committed to the intention behind the Erase-the-Tape technique as part of the original healing program you read to yourself earlier in this chapter, so you don't ever have to do that again.

Now, affirm that you intend to erase every thought, feeling, desire, assumption, belief, and so on about the incident or incidents within your circle.

Step 3: Count It Down

Count down, slowly, from 10 to 0, repeating your cue word 10 to 15 times after each number. Remember that 10 represents the present moment and 0 represents the moment that the issue in question first became a problem for you. By Erasing the Tape on everything in between, you can start out fresh.

Looking at the things in your circle, get a good mental grip on them. Then, with eyes either open or closed, count down, repeating your cue word 10 to 15 times between numbers. For example, again use "bliss" as the cue word:

> "10 ... bliss bliss bliss bliss bliss bliss ... 9 ... bliss bliss bliss
> bliss bliss ... 8 ... bliss bliss bliss bliss bliss bliss ..." and so
> on, all the way down to zero

When you reach zero, take a big breath in and blow it out forcefully with a whoosh! This will help any remaining negative energy around the problem to exit.

Step 4: Final Clearing Statements

Finish the clearing portion of ETT by affirming:

> "I clear all the ways I'm holding any of this in my body, or anywhere else." (Repeat your cue.)

> "I clear all the patterns connected to all these ways." (Repeat your cue.)

> "I clear all the emotions connected to all these patterns." (Repeat your cue.)

Step 5: Install Whatever You Desire

Next, install whatever you like to replace what you've just erased. If you're stuck on what to install, I suggest focusing on the opposite of what you erased. For example, if you erased anger, install self-acceptance or love. If you erased a betrayal, install love and trust. You can install positive qualities individually or as a bundle. I like to install bundles of positive qualities. I first visualize a circle in front of me and then put the various qualities into it, finally stepping into the circle myself. To install positive qualities, count up from 0—representing the moment the issue first became a problem for you—to 10, the present moment; repeat your cue word after each number.

That's it; you're done. How do you feel? Be sure to record your progress in your Bliss Journal. Enjoy!

PRACTICE NOTES ON ERASING THE TAPE

For some issues you may need to Erase the Tape more than once to complete your healing. That's perfectly okay; just be sure to note your SUDS rating, or emotional intensity about the issue, as you proceed through each countdown. If you find you need to Erase the Tape on an issue more than once, it's a good thing—it means you've got a tiger by the tail, and it's finally releasing its hold on you. Keep going! The ZPoint bonus, as I call it—the feeling of deep relaxation experienced after completing the ZPoint Process—will be both your reward and your guide. Press on until you no longer feel any negativity or tension at all when you think about the issue. After Erasing the Tape, I always try to summon up the issue's negativity again by repeating the names of people involved, visualizing incidents, and remembering the situation's feelings of anger, shame, or guilt. When none of these upsets me even an iota, I know I'm finished.

As you count backward, you may find that more thoughts about the subject you're working on surface. As new thoughts surface, write them down in your Bliss Journal for a future session of ETT practice. Keep at it—and keep enjoying the deep relaxation of ZPoint—until you feel all layers of the problem have been cleared.

Don't forget to record your ZPoint practice in your Bliss Journal—describe what you worked on and the outcomes you received. In your outcomes, also detail how much relaxation and mental clarity you achieved. The more you practice ZPoint, the clearer your thoughts will become and the more relaxed you will be.

CHAPTER 8

Putting It All Together: First Steps

*Y*ou've now learned EFT, TAT, and ZPoint; the A.M. Energizing and P.M. Harmonizing routines; and a lot of quick practices designed to relax and calm you throughout your day. You know what bliss means for *you*, and you have a Bliss List and Shadow List. What next?

First, you need to do some groundwork before using the energy therapies you've learned to any great extent. Your mind will naturally come up with all sorts of reasons as to why they won't work: "It's too weird," "This is too simple to really work," "It's a bunch of bull; I don't believe any of it." Every energy coach and therapist out there has heard

This chapter relates to phases 1, 6, and 7 of the Everyday Bliss Process, outlined on pages 9, 11, and 12.

the whole gamut of these reasons. Honor your feelings—and then use the following process to get past them so that the therapies you've learned can be uniquely effective for you.

INITIAL WORK TO DO

Larry Nims, creator of Be Set Free Fast, an excellent though complex intentional therapy, proposes a great set of initial issues to do clearings on (2000). Any one of these issues can stand in the way of your ability to use the energy therapies successfully; your first priority should be to address this list. Please don't skip this step—do these clearings *first*, before tackling more pressing problems. You can use any of the energy therapies you've now learned to address these issues. You may not feel as though you have all of these issues; still, since you can clear them so quickly, do them all.

- "I don't deserve to find my bliss (be relaxed, healthy, etc.)."

- "I can't find my bliss; I never have before."

- "I'm not smart enough to live a blissful lifestyle."

- "If I find my bliss, it will hurt someone I love."

- "I am afraid that _____ (fill in whatever energy therapy technique you're using) won't work for me." Alternatively, "I doubt that...."

- "I am afraid that these clearings won't last."

- "I doubt that they will work."

- "I don't trust myself to do this right."

- "I doubt I can change and make it stick."

- "Some part of me is actively preventing me from changing (getting well, becoming relaxed, more healthy, in bliss, etc.)."

Do an additional clearing for any anger you might have toward yourself about the problems that you have. Make it a point to incorporate a treatment for self-directed anger, intolerance, or other negative feelings in every session of energy therapy you do. A few words is all it takes. In ZPoint, for example, you might say, "I clear all the ways I am intolerant of my own mistakes and mad at myself for having all these problems..." and then repeat your cue word 10 to 15 times.

As Nims points out in his workshops, it's important to forgive yourself for having problems. Forgive yourself for hurting others because of the problems you have. Forgive yourself for hurting yourself. Mean it. Sincere forgiveness will attract a wealth of gifts, blessings, and resources for you.

"But It's Not Working for Me!" or "It Was Working but Now It Isn't!"

When you're having difficulty getting a technique to work for you—or feel confused, frightened, or upset—try this simple energy correction before applying an energy therapy to the problem again. If your energy is reversed (you may experience this as feeling fuzzy-headed, clumsy, and unable to connect the dots in your day), energy therapies may not work as well. If this is the case, do the following Belly Button Correction every day, several times a day. This practice will retrain your body's energy system. (This correction can be helpful even for those who don't exhibit any signs of energetic disorganization as it sends a strong, clearing pulse through all of the body's energy meridians.)

THE BELLY BUTTON CORRECTION

1. Place the index finger of one hand lengthwise across your upper lip, its thumb lengthwise across the ball of your chin. Place the fingertips of your other hand in a circle around your belly button; press in gently. As you do, rub your upper lip and chin briskly with the sides of your index finger and thumb for ten seconds. Switch hands and repeat.

2. While keeping the fingertips of one hand pressed in around the belly button, place the index finger and thumb of your other hand on your Collarbone points (see illus-

tration on page 103); rub these vigorously for ten seconds. Switch hands and repeat.

3. While keeping the fingertips of one hand pressed in around the belly button, place your other hand behind you, just above your tailbone (coccyx); rub vigorously for ten seconds. Switch hands and repeat.

4. Take a deep breath; release.

Repeat this whole routine as necessary. Trust your body, it will tell you what it needs.

Benchmarking Your Bliss

To know if you're getting where you want to be, it's helpful to set *benchmarks*. Benchmarks are subgoals that help you know if you're on track to your larger goal. If your larger goal is to have an hour each day to call your own and you're starting out with ten minutes, a good subgoal might be, "In a month I will have twenty-five minutes, three times a week to call my own." Looking at a larger goal can be daunting and can stymie our efforts before they even start. When we have benchmarks to compare our progress to, attaining the large goal becomes a reasonable undertaking. Whichever you prefer, large goals or small ones, create your benchmarks accordingly.

Just as you have in other segments of the Everyday Bliss Process, limit your subgoals to three per larger goal so as not to overwhelm yourself. To be extra good to yourself, work on no more than three such subgoals at any one time. This is one place where slow and steady really does do the job best. Here's how:

1. Choose one of your bliss goals to accomplish. (Do the following process for each of the large goals you're working on. As you accomplish each large goal and it drops off your list, add another large goal.)

2. Decide what three subgoals you need to accomplish to know that you're progressing toward your larger goal.

3. Put these subgoals on a reasonable timeline. What's a reasonable amount of time? It's as long as you think it's going to take, plus a few days leeway on either side to allow for the unexpected. It's important not to negatively judge your time allotments. Don't tell yourself your benchmarks "should" take less time, or you "should" be as speedy at accomplishing goals as your friends. No comparisons! Give yourself the luxury of not feeling pressed. This is a pathway to bliss, after all.

Note in your Bliss Journal how you feel as a result of accomplishing these subgoals and overall goals. Less stressed? More relaxed? Jot your experiences down—you're creating a powerful map that will provide you with directions should you ever get lost and need to find your way back to bliss.

Choice Paralysis and Its Cure

Sometimes having lots of items to choose from can cause *choice paralysis*, a condition where you're so flooded with options you can make no move at all. Choice paralysis can make embracing your everyday bliss tough. It's great if your Bliss List is twenty items long—this will give you many self-nurturing items to choose from. But sometimes lots of choices can bog us down. We can end up always thinking the right answer is to be found over the next hill, in the next few items on our list, or by taking just one more course. Paralyzed by our many possible choices, we then choose nothing or something less than best.

Defeating choice paralysis is simple. Take out your Bliss List (or in other situations, your list of options) and give yourself to the count of ten to see what item jumps off the page at you. No thinking allowed. Take the item that acts the most like a new puppy—the one that jumps into your lap and begs you to take it home, crying, "Me! Choose me!"

If you tend to experience buyer's remorse and find yourself always thinking about the other choices you could have made, realize that this is a personal gremlin of self-doubt. It's haunting you because at some point in time you were told—or shown by example—not to trust your instincts. Pay it no mind. Take the TAT pose (see illustration on page 117) for a moment and affirm that this choice (and indeed, any choice you make) is what is good for you right now. In the TAT pose, give gratitude for having the time, space, and ability to choose. What a wonderful life you live!

Wasn't that simple? Now go ahead and decide what three things you'd like to do tomorrow to feel relaxed and blissful. Jot down a quick note to yourself on what fun you're going to have tomorrow and put it somewhere you'll see it first thing in the morning. For me, that's on the bathroom mirror. If you, like me, tend to acclimate to changes in your surroundings after a few days, you may want to move your notification spot around—just make it a place you'll be sure to see before you gear up for the day. Go ahead, stick your note up now. I'll wait.

Regaining Peace of Mind

Is your note all set for tomorrow? Great. Now we can delve into the juicy stuff: how to start chipping away at the issues that keep your energy bound up in knots. Once these knots of negative energy are unraveled, you'll find yourself bounding around with energy to spare. Unraveling these knots is easy, but it does take a bit of dedication and effort to get started. Gary Craig (2006), creator of EFT, was the first to put a name to using energy therapy in this way. He calls it the "Personal Peace Process." My version of the Personal Peace Process will help you rid yourself of the far-reaching negative effects of unsettling incidents. No matter how small, you can address them with this process and your choice of EFT, TAT, or ZPoint.

THE PERSONAL PEACE PROCESS

1. If you haven't already expanded your Shadow List as described in chapter 5, now is the time to do so. Add to your Shadow List every upsetting, unsettling, or negative incident you can remember. Go as far back as you can.

Some incidents will be from childhood, others from later years. Don't be surprised if you have fifty, a hundred, or even a couple of hundred upsetting incidents. Most people will—this is normal.

2. Write down everything that comes to mind, even if you're not experiencing a particularly bad or negative feeling when you think about the event. The mere fact that you remembered it means that something is there. Write it down.

3. These types of incidents often play over and over again in your mind. Use that. Give each negative incident a descriptive movie title. Examples from childhood traumas that have survived to the present day might be: *Mrs. Macdonald Told the Whole Class My Terrible Grade on the History Test, Anna Betrayed Our Friendship,* or *Mom Yelled at Me When It Was Really Susan's Fault.*

4. When you have your list, choose the biggest, most upsetting of these incidents and clear it with the energy therapy of your choice. If you don't experience any intensity of negative feeling (a SUDS of 0) on an event that you nevertheless remember as negative, you may be repressing your feelings or have only partially cleared its effects. Do ten full clearings, using any of the energy methods, on every possible aspect of this "low intensity" incident.

As we learned in chapter 5, breaking an incident down into its different components or aspects is a great way to identify the relevant feelings to work on. The following is an example from one of my coaching clients, Lynn, a team leader and systems designer at an IT firm. Even though she came into the session terming the incident described as "no big deal," she wasn't sleeping, had difficulty making decisions, and suffered a constantly sour stomach, so we knew something was there. This is her movie of the incident:

Title: *The Chairman of the Board Said My Idea Was Stupid*

SUDS Intensity: "It was an off day, no big deal really. I'd give it a SUDS of three or so."

Scene 1: "I was a few seconds late to the board meeting and I could see Garth, the chairman, was pissed off the second I stepped in the door. I knew I was in for it."

Scene 2: "Garth dressed me down in front of the reps from Sumitech. I just died inside."

Scene 3: "I apologized to both Garth and Mr. Ota from Sumitech, but I hated doing it and was completely embarrassed. My whole face was red."

Scene 4: "I still had to make my presentation halfway through the meeting, but by now my heart had gone out of it. I had a great presentation—my team said it was the best we had to put forward—but I knew before I even started that I was going to mess it up. When Garth started tapping his fingers on the table, I completely lost my concentration."

Scene 5: "Garth said my team's ideas were the poorest they'd seen. I felt stunned. I hated the fact that I didn't have a snappy comeback. I felt completely screwed and sat through the rest of the meeting fuming. I'm so disappointed in myself. And I can't stand Garth!"

Now *that's* clarity! After making this movie, Lynn reported an adjusted SUDS of 9.5. Dividing an incident into separate scenes really pulls the dregs of negative energy out of their deepest hiding places. Treat each of these scenes as its own incident. Apply EFT, TAT, or ZPoint to these scenes, one by one, and you'll feel the negative charge drain clean away.

5. Clear at least one movie a day for at least three months. Since it only takes a few minutes to clear a movie, you may want to do two or three a day. Three months is ninety days. If you keep at it steadily, that's ninety negative incidents cleared—a huge chunk of what's keeping your available energy bound up in knots.

Relish the relaxation and bliss you feel as you clear these incidents and their knots unwind. Once the knots have unwound, notice the increased energy you enjoy and the sense of calm that pervades your everyday affairs. Your mind will begin to feel clear, expansive, and at rest.

Notice how much better your body feels—how your muscles, once tightly clenched, have softened and are now more at ease than ever before. Note, too, how much higher your threshold for getting upset is. Things just don't bother you the way they once did. Enjoy your improved relationships and the fact that many of your therapy-type issues just aren't there any more.

If you want to test the process, go ahead and call up some of the movies you made of the troubling incidents you cleared. Notice once again how even incidents that were previously quite intense have faded into a stoic "Yep, that did happen, but I don't know why I was so upset—it's no big deal." Enjoy the fact that you mean it.

Note any improvements in your blood pressure, pulse, and breathing ability in your Bliss Journal. You now have many pieces of evidence that you can—and do—experience bliss, daily.

CHAPTER 9

Situational and Instantaneous Bliss Generators

*W*hen you lead a busy life, it can be difficult to find the time to embark on longer bliss practices. In this chapter we'll explore bliss generators that will instantly take you out of negativity.

Once you have a good handle on the Personal Peace Process and are seeing results, you'll want to move from the past into the present. When you're busy, it can be difficult to recognize the bliss that already exists in your life. Knowing how to stretch time in a meditative way can

This chapter relates to phases 6 and 7 of the Everyday Bliss Process, outlined on pages 11 and 12.

be useful not only in inducing bliss, but also in becoming more aware of its presence. The following exercise teaches you to do just that—my clients love it.

WAKING UP TO THE PRESENT MOMENT

1. Sit at your personal altar or similar quiet space and, with conscious intent, turn your attention to the now.

2. Register all that is happening around you. Focus on the many different sounds you hear: birdsong, a plane over-head, the hum of a fan, your own bones creaking, the soft whoosh of breath, the ticking of a clock, children playing outside.... Realize that by the time you have listed all of these to yourself, the moment has changed and you are in a different now.

3. Rest your eyes gently, focus soft. What do you see? The many twists and turns of a painting, a random sock strewn on the floor, motes of dust hanging and turning in the air, a shaft of sunlight illuminating the pattern of the carpet.... Realize that by the time you have listed all of these to yourself, the moment has changed and you are in a different now.

4. Turn your attention inward. What do you feel? The stretching of the quads in your left leg, sweat running down your neck, an itch on your right forefinger, the breath filling your nostrils and lungs, a sense of heaviness in the

abdomen…. Realize that by the time you have listed all of these to yourself, the moment has changed and you are in a different now.

5. When you have brought your mindful awareness to what composes your space—both inner and outer—draw a circle in your mind. Locate the circle a few feet in front of you and put all of the things you've noticed into it. Right now, you are outside the circle, symbolically akin to how we experience ourselves as "outside of" the present moment.

6. Now, ZPoint-style, affirm, "I clear all the ways I am asleep to the full experience of the present moment" and "I clear all the ways I disconnect myself from the now." Use whatever words are meaningful to you. Also clear the reasons, emotions, and patterns that are preventing you from living fully in the now.

7. Now, count these down, from 10 to 0, while repeating your cue word. You'll find that in this particular Erase-the-Tape session, the things in your circle do not fade, but actually become more solid.

8. When you've reached zero, step your whole body into your imaginary circle and sit, stand, or lie down in it. Choose whatever posture you find comfortable. Be present with all of the things in your awareness.

9. Make a positive affirmation, such as, "I am continually aware of the present moment. I live in the now." You may not be fully aware of the present moment yet, but in affirming that you are, you will begin to approach that state.

10. Count upward from 0 to 10. You may find that the things inside your circle either sink into your body/mind or fade away entirely as they become facets of your continuing awareness. Whatever changes you observe will be unique to you. These will be the harbingers of your increased awareness.

Repeat as necessary—and enjoy!

PEACE GENERATOR AND SHARING YOUR WEALTH

I love to use energy therapies in slightly unconventional ways. The following is something you can do, in addition to the TAT you may be doing, to bring even more peace into your heart. I originally created this process for a client who was finding it difficult to be the executor of a relative's will because the other relatives insisted on squabbling. You can imagine the stress this kind of situation can create. Whatever contentious situation you find yourself in, the following process will work to balance your energy, bring immense peace and love into your heart, and reground you. Already present within you is a wealth of resources to help and heal you. The following process will teach you how to multiply these resources by sharing them. Remember the old saying: love divided is love multiplied.

GENERATING PEACE

1. Meditate on what resource or help you need *now* to get through this negative situation with calm, peace of mind, and mental groundedness.

2. Holding the TAT pose, say, "God/spirit/universe (or whatever your concept of a higher power is), I ask for what I need now, right now, to let me feel peace in the midst of all this chaos and anger." You can either ask for something specific here or simply open yourself to all possibilities.

    When you sincerely ask something of your higher power, you always receive an immediate and positive response. Whether or not you understand or are even able to recognize that response depends on how you proceed from here. (For a great resource to help you with this step and what you're dealing with, check out the movie *The Secret*. I highly recommend it to all my clients who are in the midst of negativity and need to generate positive behavior, resources, and situations in their lives *right now*.)

3. Still holding the TAT pose, open yourself to truly receiving the help given. This is more difficult than it may

appear, for you cannot receive if you are in a position of frustration, anger, or negativity of any kind.

How, then, can you get into the proper frame of mind? Use what I call a *gratitude rosary*. This isn't a real set of beads; it's a sequence of thoughts focused on gratitude. To construct a gratitude rosary, take a break from the TAT pose and make a list of things you are truly, intensely grateful for. Think you don't have much to be grateful for? Think again. If you have any good relationships—with a spouse, parent, child, best friend, teacher, pet, or anyone else—list them. If you have a roof over your head and food in your belly on a continual basis, list that, too. Be sure to write down the fact that you have breath in your body and your health—whatever state of health you're in, it could be worse. Give thanks for what you've got, even if it isn't perfect.

No matter how bleak the outlook at this particular moment, you are profoundly blessed. Pause to reflect on how very fortunate you are—there are many people living on the streets with no food, holes in their clothing, and no place to go when it rains or is cold. There are people who have no one to love them and who have never been told what a bright shining star they are. Include on your list anyone who has ever loved you and/or given you encouraging messages, even once. Include strangers who have exclaimed over your nice haircut or thanked you for a great speech you gave. Ditto that person next door whom you don't really know, but who always waves when you pass. Love is all around you and it comes in many guises. Open your eyes. Truly, you are blessed.

Keep adding "beads" to your gratitude rosary until you have at least ten or more things you are *intensely* grateful for. When you are out of sorts, you are out of alignment with the energy flow of the universe. Consciously being grateful will get you back into alignment. Use this gratitude rosary whenever you are feeling small, put-upon, or at the mercy of life's changes.

4. While in the TAT pose, remember slowly what each gratitude bead stands for, giving deep and genuine thanks for the presence of these blessings in your life as you list them one by one. As you count, peace will flood back into your soul and the resources you asked for will come winging to you. Some resources will come to you right now, but they will also continue to filter in for the next few days or even weeks.

   Continue this practice as long as you like or until a feeling of profound relaxation steals over you, relaxing every muscle and quieting the mind. Drink lots of water and breathe deeply. Breathe in your blessings.

5. You can stop at this point, or you can choose to share your resources to benefit everyone in the situation— and perhaps resolve it even more quickly. To share your resources, find the place in your body where the necessary resources are located. Put your hand over that place, and then, as if you were pulling a toy out of a box, draw some

of this energy out of you and hold it in your hand. See, feel, hear, and smell the energy taking shape in your hand. What does it look like? How does it feel? What color is it? Does it have a scent?

This energy "resource packet" might take the form of a flower, a stone, or something from nature; it might be a book, an animal, or a band of color; it might sound like a musical note or smell like cinnamon—it's all up to you. For example, let's say that the resource needed is peace. When you think about peace and the people who bring peace into your life, an energy packet will develop. Let's say that in this instance, this packet takes the shape of a beautiful red rose and you feel it in your heart center. Reach into your heart and hold in your hand this red rose.

6. Now that your resource packet has taken shape in your hand, call the energy of the main individuals involved in this situation into your space. Imagine them standing in front of you. One by one—and with gratitude for all they are teaching you—hand each person a rose (you may need to create a bouquet!); watch peace wash over each face.

Now, and this is a crucial point, to do this, you have to really, really, *really* be ready to share your peace-giving resources with them. If you're not ready yet, do TAT on your unwillingness. Being willing to share means that you have no further negative investment in a situation.

7. When you have given a resource packet to everyone in the situation, affirm that you still have resources for yourself—that the rose is still sitting safely in your heart center.

8. Hold the TAT pose while saying thank you to the others involved in the situation, and then thank yourself for being willing to grow. (And really mean it, too!)

9. You're finished. Drink water and rest. You may also wish to take a nap. You may need it—your neurology is literally recoding itself to draw peace and resolution into your life.

Be pleasantly surprised by the amazing changes that happen both in yourself and in others involved in this formerly contentious situation. People tell me all the time that after using this process, wonderful things have happened—the aunt they were fighting with suddenly called them to apologize, the boss who had always been nasty made overtures of kindness, the partner they were butting heads with suddenly made a turnaround. Whether or not you experience this level of change, this is a great little process—it doesn't take long, and you'll feel concrete benefits to your own health and wellness immediately.

CREATING AN OUTRAGEOUSLY COMPELLING OUTCOME

Have you ever wondered why you don't get what you want? The reason may be because you don't know why you want the thing, what the outcome of having it will be, when (or indeed sometimes if) you are really willing to make any necessary changes, and who might be affected by your getting the thing you want (which can create its own interesting situations). These who-what-where-when-why questions are the basic motivators behind achieving our desires. If you don't know the answers to these questions, you may not get what you want.

If lack of clarity prevents you from achieving the goals you desire, use the following process to ensure success. Apply this process to all of your "I wanna" agenda items to transform them into ironclad "I will absolutely accomplish this objective" items instead. The following eight steps will give you a personalized action plan that you'll be able to follow effortlessly and with unwavering intensity.

It's important to follow all of the steps of this simple process. Strong timelining (below) is especially important, as this is where most people go off the rails when trying to accomplish their goals.

Step 1: What Do You Want?

Red or blue? Long or short? Full-time or half-time? Fifty thousand dollars or a cool million? Being as specific as possible, describe what you want using all of the ways you represent success in this situation to yourself: visually, or how you see the achievement of this goal; kinesthetically, or how you feel the achievement of this goal inside; and aurally, or how you hear the achievement of this goal through what you yourself and others say.

Step 2: What Else Will Change When You Attain Your Goal?

Think environment, relationships, time effects, energy flows, and so on. When one area of our life changes, other areas can suddenly change, too. Carefully consider how your goal may affect other areas of your life.

Step 3: Who Else Will Be Affected?

Start with your most intimate relationships—significant others, family, children, friends—and then extend your focus to your larger community. Many people see this as a negative effect and go looking for who will be upset by their changing. While this is certainly a reaction to consider, I urge you to consider the positive effects your change will have. For every action, there is an equal and opposite reaction. For every negative, a positive. What changes in others will ripple out from your own change?

Step 4: What Resources Do You Already Have?

Think in terms of time, equipment, money, education/training, and personal or financial support. What's already there—perhaps just lying around on your metaphorical table—that can help you accomplish this goal?

Step 5: Do You Need Any Other Resources to Achieve Your Goal?

What's missing? What else do you need to have before you can achieve the goal at hand? This could be anything from further research to bolstered courage to an actual tool of some kind. Figure out how to obtain whatever resources you need to continue toward your goal.

Step 6: Is Achieving This Goal Within Your Control?

Be realistic. "Some day when I have more _____." (money, training, time, etc.) means you can't do the thing now. Is achieving your goal—right now, today, or within a reasonable space of time—within your control? If not, what needs to change in order for it to become within your control?

Step 7: Will Anyone Object?

It's not necessary to have the full compliance of everyone in your sphere to make a needed change. Sometimes others may desperately want the old you back. This is a normal human response. Allow your loved ones to give you reasonable reality checks, but don't let their needs pull you back into outmoded ways of behaving or being. Whether others make their acceptance of the new you easy on themselves is entirely their own choice.

Step 8: Timelining Your Goal for Complete Success

Timelining is the final key to achieving tough goals, time after time—it's also something people typically either forget about or choose to disregard. But if you don't give your goal a deadline, it could end up dead in the water. Here's how to do it.

After completing the seven steps above, ask yourself, "What is my first action toward achieving this goal or outcome *now*?" If that means picking up the phone book and hiring someone to clean your house while you acquire the new training that will let you accomplish your goal, then that's your first step. Think ahead to next week. What comes next in the process? And next? Write down three to five things to do next week. Think even further ahead, to the very end of the process. See yourself as having accomplished the desired outcome, and then reverse the process. Ask yourself, "What did I do the minute/day/week before I ended up here at my goal?" I like to start with what I was doing ten minutes before I achieved the goal and then work my way back a month or so.

Now, put both the beginning steps and the ending steps on a timeline. Assign your goal a date of completion and work out where halfway through the process will be. Repeat the above process with this new "halfway to the finish line" time period. Let's say you have a goal that will take a year to accomplish. What will you accomplish from the start to the six-month mark? Go through the process again until you've identified several of the steps that lead up to the halfway point. Now you have three points with detailed descriptions on your timeline.

Finally, add this information to your calendar. Note down the beginning, middle, and end points of your timeline, as well as the tasks to be done in the weeks preceding and following each. This will generate a simple daily to-do list; for maximal success, keep this to no more than three action items. As you proceed along your timeline, always look forward to the next few days or weeks to provide you with new tasks to add to your list.

For example, if beginning a year-long project on January 1, in February assess the work you accomplished during the previous month. Next, look forward four months to June and ask yourself, "What is it going to take *today* to get me there?" This will help you fill in your entire calendar so that you never have a day where you don't know what to work on and will always know exactly where you are in the process. Simple!

What about when you don't—or can't—make a deadline? When this happens, just pick up where you left off and keep going. Let the whole process shift a day, week, or however long is necessary. But if you're procrastinating, don't treat the delay lightly: do extra work with the energy therapy of your choice on the roots of the problem.

LET YOUR ENVIRONMENT EVOLVE YOU—EFFORTLESSLY

Evolutionary environments are those that pull us forward into new places. The process above created an environment that enabled you to draw peace into your life and bring calm resolution to a contentious situation. You created a new environment of gratitude, love, and resourcefulness. This is a great example of creating a total environment for bliss in your life. If you're having difficulty putting routines into practice—or the thought of taking time out to do things on your lists feels oppressive—you can create both physical and mental environments that will naturally support your continuous improvement, no matter what else you do or don't do. When you surround yourself with people, situations, and things that stretch and support you, you'll evolve naturally and effortlessly. And when you change your *internal* environment—the only thing you truly have real control over—the impossible can become real. How does this happen? Let's look at an example.

Early in her leadership career, Kay Cannon (www.leadership whisperer.com), the current president of the International Coach Federation, was the VP of operations for a national healthcare company. There she experienced near-constant political upheaval and culture change, such that "Everyday I went to work knowing there was going to be a battle. And I knew there would be, figuratively, blood all over the floor. The only thing I never knew was whose blood it was going to be—mine or somebody else's." This negative external environment influenced her own behavior. One employee called her a "cold, heartless bitch of a boss." But then, after one of her employees died and stress-induced heart palpitations made Kay sink to the floor in pain, she made the conscious decision to change her environment by changing herself. When she left the company fifteen years later, one employee remarked, "There goes the heart and soul of this company. It'll never be the same."

That's some change! And it came simply from Kay's contouring of her internal environment to bring herself into better alignment with her life mission and everyday bliss.

Create Your Own Evolutionary Environment

Let's create an evolutionary environment. Think about something you would like to have in your life. It could be a state of mind, membership in an organization, better communication with others, a better position at work, complete inner peace, anything.

Now consider this: what has to happen—inside of you or outside of you—so that this change you desire will occur naturally, without any other effort on your part? For example, if peace of mind is your goal, what changes or shifts can you make in your mind, body, relationships, and physical surroundings so that peace of mind will come naturally to you? What changes can you make to your mental environment so that you'll find yourself guided automatically to the right actions, situations, and relationships to achieve your goal? What questions can you ask yourself to internally attract the goal? Which of your relationships will further your goal and support your process?

Have you ever said, "If I had a million dollars, of course I could _____!"? Well, if you had that money, what would you buy to make your environment as evolutionary as possible? Or maybe what you need is something you can't buy, like a new set of friends. If so, set about finding new friends through interest groups, social networking events, and other venues. What about a different place to live? A new job? Start searching the classifieds. And don't let yourself opt out—avoid thoughts like, "Oh, it would be too much work to find a new position in this economy" or "Packing's a bummer." If you really need a new job or new place to live, leverage your networks and hop to it. No time like the present!

Creating an environment that will pull you forward is an exercise in reflection and consideration. It's often helpful to discuss this process—and its many questions—with a friend, coach, or significant other. Such people can be part of the evolutionary environment you create. *Mastermind groups*—likeminded people who gather for mutual support—can also be tremendously helpful in providing feedback and objective perspective. In fact, I highly suggest that you either start or join your own mastermind group as a way to support your ongoing journey to bliss.

The Everyday Bliss Mastermind Group Experience

To create an environment that will help you evolve using the principles and tools mentioned in this book, consider either starting or joining an Everyday Bliss mastermind group. In doing so, you will not only help yourself, you'll also help others who need the Everyday Bliss experience.

Mastermind groups are a special type of group designed to support catalytic change, transformation, and enlightenment in people's lives. The power of many minds together is far greater than any individual mind, and considering others' perspectives can give you more flexibility in your approaches to bliss.

You can participate in a mastermind group wherever you are, whether in person, at your home or a café, or virtually, using a free telephone bridgeline and bulletin board system. I personally belong to three different mastermind groups; these are indispensable to me. No one person runs a mastermind group; rather, a group runs itself, with each person getting equal time to discuss concerns and receive input.

Here's an abbreviated description of how to run an Everyday Bliss mastermind group:

1. Decide how you want your group to work. For example, your group might:

   - Go through this book, from beginning to end, working through exercises together.

   - Focus collectively on using the Bliss Blockers and Bliss Keys.

   - Concentrate on one energy therapy: tapping, holding the TAT pose, or using cue words on a list of issues generated by the group.

   - Act as an energy pool for members, through trading time and services (e.g., babysitting, shopping, etc.).

   - Cooperatively explore other ways of cultivating daily bliss.

- Pursue a combination of the above.

2. Decide what kind of membership focus you want in your group. When the membership of a group is focused around a commonality—such as a particular interest, age range, profession, or geographical area—members are often able to do energy work together more easily because their minds already share a common groove. Also, develop a short list of the personal qualities you're looking for in members—for example, being open to change, willing to learn, committed to keeping the group's confidence, dedicated to personal peace, and so on.

3. Put an ad for your group in local community centers, grocery-store bulletin boards, churches, yoga studios, local government offices, and on websites.

4. Collect your group until you have six to twelve people, and set a date for your first meeting. You can meet in person—at a home, café, or local community center—or virtually, using a free telephone bridgeline. (One such longstanding and stable service is www.freeconference.com.)

5. Decide on your schedule of meetings, who is to host which meetings where, and topics for each meeting. Stick to your schedule and keep supporting each other.

The best way to know what an Everyday Bliss mastermind group is like is to participate in one. If there are no groups near you, visit this book's website (www.everydaybliss.org) for help with setting up your own group. If there is a group near you, e-mail the group leaders today. Don't wait—a mastermind group will help your strong, wonderful self to grow even stronger!

EXTRA RESOURCE

I've created a special area on everydaybliss.org for you to gather, form, and manage your own Everyday Bliss mastermind group. This space and its tools are available to you as a free resource—use it to connect, enhance, and maintain your inner peace. In the free mastermind area, you'll find a much expanded set of how-to's, a place to register your Everyday Bliss mastermind group so new members can find you, and free, multi-party telephone bridge lines you can use. Come on over!

CHAPTER 10

Preventive Maintenance and Extending the Field of Bliss

$\mathcal{I}$n this chapter we'll explore how to extend the preventive maintenance you've already learned (in the A.M./P.M. energy routines and the Personal Peace Process) in other ways to achieve a stable emotional and energy equilibrium throughout your day. Remember how we're all surrounded by fields of energy? In this chapter, you'll also learn how to leverage your energy field to extend your own feeling of relaxation and calm to those you interact with. My life mission is to reduce stress, increase bliss, and enable individuals to heal both themselves and their loved ones. Creating bliss fields is how we're going to do it, so let's start there!

This chapter relates to phases 6 and 7 of the Everyday Bliss Process, outlined on pages 11 and 12.

An Experiment in Expanding Your Field Effect

This experiment starts with just one key rule: revel in the fun of sharing your bliss. Choose a person to practice on who doesn't know you'll be sending them a little bit of happiness. I like to practice on strangers who are upset—in line at the post office or bank, deep in their own issues and yelling inappropriately at their kids, or visibly sad or depressed. You can do this experiment anywhere you happen to be. Your field of energy is infinite, so you don't need to be physically close to the person—you can even send bliss to someone in another country. To start out with, though, choose someone close enough for you to observe the effects.

First, generate a feeling of bliss within yourself. Call to mind someone who loves you and bask in the glow of that love. Get nice and relaxed; feel goodwill to all. This is your starting point.

Next, because it's never okay to do anything to or for anyone without their permission, affirm that you are sending energy to the other person's higher self. Higher selves know how to channel incoming energy. If it's *not* good for a person to feel more relaxed or blissful right now, the person's higher self won't accept the energy you send.

Now, begin to radiate the peaceful, blissful feeling you have within yourself outward toward your practice partner. If it's someone who is upset, note their reactions and keep radiating. Send energy to this person for up to five minutes. Sometimes the effects of this will be immediately apparent; sometimes they will take a while to develop. In some cases they won't develop before you have to go on your way. Nonetheless, by expanding your own field of bliss outward, you have done good work, which will return to you in the form of more blissful interactions with others in general. Keep at it. Send energy to three people each day. This is a form of giving back, or energy tithing. And as you know, the more you give, the more comes back to you. Note what happens in your Bliss Journal.

Start sending out bliss whenever you are in a contentious situation, such as an office meeting or an argument with your partner or child. As you increase your awareness of the potential for bliss in the situations that surround you, it's also important to become more aware of the flow of negative energy. Negative energy that flows between human beings can create a feedback loop that will collect more and more negative energy. It is this kind of feedback loop that often runs the show in arguments, causing both parties to become angrier and say and do increasingly hurtful things. Eckhart Tolle describes this feedback loop as the greedy sucking neediness of the *Pain-Body* that all human beings have in common (1999). (The Pain-Body, built of all the negative experiences you've ever had, is the structure you break down when you do the Personal Peace Process.) If you can generate and send out good, blissful energy during a contentious situation, you have an excellent chance of ending any ugliness right then and there.

As you add this kind of charitable giving to your daily bliss practice, your environment will begin to radically change for the better. Arguments simply won't be able to find you. Angry people will avoid you or calm instantly in your presence. The calamities that once befell you—the accidents, illnesses, and unpleasant turns of fate—begin to fade slowly into the distance. Those around you will comment that you seem to lead a charmed life. And you will. It can take a lot of practice to achieve this, but it's worth it. And, if all of us practice this kind of selfless giving, the world will be a much happier and more loving place.

EXTENDING THE BLISS FIELD IN YOUR EVENING HOURS

Dealing with the hustle-bustle of evening and weekend social commitments while managing your energy can be a daunting task. You'll want to arrive home, therefore, with all the goodness and sweetness you can possibly muster. To do this, you first need to shake off the day.

My client Aiko is the managing director of a major West Coast ballet company. She finds her job more stressful than anything else she's ever done. Before she was introduced to the Everyday Bliss Process, Aiko was crying in her car every night before she drove home. We turned this around with Everyday Bliss coaching and the following simple little exercise. This exercise is an excellent relaxer to do in your car (only while parked, please!), after work but before you go home.

THE IN-CAR CORE DUMP

First, choose where to conduct this de-stressing ritual. Ideally this should be some midway point between work and home, such as the parking lot of your workplace. Keep an icon in your car that you can use to store all of the frustration and stress accumulated during your workday. This could be a rag doll, figurine, or knickknack; in Aiko's case it's a car air freshener in the shape of a dove. Do ten P.M. Cross Crawls (as described on page 90) and a Triple Thump Plus, as described in chapter 4.

Next, take your icon in your hands and let all of your day's angst, stress, frustration, and anger drain into it. Place the icon on your windshield or hang it from your rearview mirror. The negative energies you put into it will leach out of the icon overnight; the touch of daylight, no matter how gloomy the weather, will clear the icon completely.

Now, reach your hands out to the sun (no matter where you are or how late it is, the sun is shining *somewhere*) and do the Daily Protection Sphere exercise described in chapter 2. Feel the sun's golden energy pour into the dark, shadowy areas you've just cleared. This beautiful golden light will purify and protect you from further negative energy influxes.

Take three deep breaths—roll down your window to get some fresh air—and you're done!

CHAPTER 11

Your Blissful Year

How are you feeling at this point? More relaxed? Less stressed? Excellent! Keep going. You now have a whole toolkit of blissful practices at your disposal and are starting to enjoy more peace and equilibrium. In this chapter we'll expand the work you've been doing into a plan to live a healthy, beautiful, blissful life, every day of the year.

A YEAR OF BLISS

This book is a veritable first-aid kit of processes to help and heal everything from self-defeating memories, habits, and behaviors to the extremely busy lifestyle of corporate management. Putting them all together in a cohesive way may seem daunting at first, so let's look at the first quarter of a typical year of bliss:

Month 1, Week 1

Take some time to set up a personal altar or meditation space and dedicate yourself to bliss in your life. Clarify what your life mission is and make your Bliss List and Shadow List. Start saying no to people and open up five to twenty minutes of time to be used just for you. Begin to reeducate the people in your life to treat you as you wish to be treated. Start doing three items from your Bliss List daily to deeply nurture yourself. Begin switching coffee, tea, and soda to pure filtered water.

Month 1, Week 2

Keep doing Bliss List items daily, adding a new one every few days. Begin to incorporate the A.M. Energizing and P.M. Harmonizing protocols into each day. If you don't exercise a lot, begin to take gentle walks. Don't stress about length or pushing yourself physically; just keep it happy. Shoehorn in another five to twenty minutes of time this week just for you. Keep increasing your water intake until recreational drinks (coffee, soda, etc.) are at a minimum.

Month 1, Week 3

Keep it up! Spend this week firming up your practice. Add another Bliss List item or two to those you do daily, or switch one item you're already doing for a new item from the list. Keep walking or doing some other form of exercise—aim for a few more minutes this week. Add in a supportive relaxation practice such as meditation or yoga.

Month 1, Week 4

Learn the Emotional Freedom Technique. Set aside an hour a day to practice on the issues from your Shadow List. Create more time if you wish. Keep up the rest of the practices you've been building, and keep track of your progress in your Bliss Journal.

Month 2, Week 1

Learn Tapas Acupressure Technique. Keep working daily on your Shadow List; continue to track your progress in your Bliss Journal. Do TAT on the most negative relationship in your life until the negative feelings resolve into peace. Work on a different negative relationship every few days. Start indulging in more treats. Enjoy a particularly nurturing service, class, or club. This could be anything from a massage to art lessons to a hiking club. Take the weekend off.

Month 2, Week 2

Learn ZPoint Process. Begin using ZPoint on your Shadow List. Do the regular protocol for the first four days, and then practice the Erase-the-Tape technique for the rest of the week. Keep releasing into bliss.... Need more time? Count it down in a ZPoint Erase-the-Tape Circle as described on page 136.

Month 2, Week 3

Bliss Journal alert: read your Bliss Journal. You should have a lot of entries on Shadow List items you've resolved. Revel in your successes—you've earned them! Even if you've only addressed one or two items with each energy therapy modality, by now you'll probably have a fair idea of which one works best for you. Devote this week to using this method to really plow through items on your Shadow List.

Month 2, Week 4

Gently increase your physical exercise (emphasis on "gently"). Continue to do Bliss List items daily and use the energy technique you're most comfortable with to practice the Personal Peace Process. Take the weekend—or one day of it—completely off to do something that will make you feel really beautiful.

Month 3, Inclusive

Keep up everything you've been doing. Now consider the people in your life. Do the Peace Generator and Sharing Your Wealth process for a week, every single day, just to see what happens. As ever, note your efforts and results in your Bliss Journal. Add more Bliss List items to your days; hire a personal trainer or take a class if that would make you feel deeply nurtured. Need more time? Add it this month. Continue on in a slow and deliberate manner. Allow your life and yourself to be expansive.

Month 4, Inclusive

Quarterly overhaul: take out your Bliss Journal and look at it again with an eye to the goals and compelling outcomes you created. How are you doing? Amend what isn't working, and keep at what is working. If you haven't already, consider creating or joining an Everyday Bliss mastermind group for extra support and nurturing.

Months 5-12, Inclusive

For the rest of the year, continue to increase your efforts to bring more time into each day and week, and more peace and comfort into your life. Keep going until you're where you need to be. Your own body and emotions will let you know if you're on track—pay attention to them, and have a wonderful, delicious, luxurious time!

When you use the Everyday Bliss Process consistently, you will reach a point where you are satisfied with your life. Your Bliss Blockers will all have been busted, and you'll no longer feel rushed or at the mercy of memories and emotions. The Bliss Keys will have given you time, space, and peace. When you reach this point, simply continue what you have been doing to maintain your practice. To further develop and even speed up this process, read some of the books in the resources section at the end of this book.

Finally, stay connected to your community and all those who create evolutionary environments for you. Keep your body and soul well-nurtured by taking regular mini-vacations; make sure you take at least one long vacation every year. Continue to generate a bliss field and spread it outward, sometimes including the whole earth in your bliss-field sharing. Teach others these methods so that they, too, can enjoy peace and bliss in their lives.

Feel blissful, every day.

CHAPTER 12

Afterword and Invitation

$\mathcal{J}$'d like to leave you with a final question: with the system outlined in this book now at your fingertips, what can you do to make your life more peaceful and more blissful? You have the tools and resources you need for a lifetime of clearing unhappiness and instilling bliss. Don't just let these tools lie fallow in the back of your head—use them! If you do, I guarantee you'll soon have more energy, peace, and pleasure in life than you know what to do with.

I'd also like to invite you to continue the connection. While the information in this book will definitely get you started, it's just the tip of the iceberg. If you'd like to continue this dialogue and immerse yourself in an evolutionary environment online, join us at:

www.everydaybliss.org

You'll find lots of resources here to support your journey to bliss, including a place for Everyday Bliss mastermind groups to gather, audios of the processes outlined here, inspiring interviews, monthly support telegatherings, and much more. Registration is free. When you register, put the phrase "blisskey5" into the special code box and you'll be taken to a private section of juicy extras just for readers to support your blissful journey.

See you there!

Resources

TECHNIQUES TAUGHT IN THIS BOOK

Emotional Freedom Technique

Craig, Gary. 2006. *The EFT Manual.* 6th ed. The Sea Ranch, CA: Self-published. To learn more about EFT, visit http://emofree.com. Also, check out the free video explaining EFT at http://everyday bliss.org/eftvideo.html.

Ball, Ron, ed. 2006. *Freedom at Your Fingertips.* Fredericksburg, VA: Inroads Publishing. I wrote "Freedom from Blockages." To access a number of different EFT bonuses donated by all the authors, visit http://everydaybliss.org/fayf.

Tapas Acupressure Technique

Fleming, Tapas 1999. *You Can Heal Now*. Redondo Beach, CA: TAT International. To learn more about TAT, visit http://tatlife.com.

ZPoint Process

Connolly, Grant. 2006. *The ZPoint Process for Instant Emotional Healing*. Revised ed. Toronto, Canada: Self-published. To learn more about the newest advances in ZPoint Process, visit http://zpointforpeace. com. Also check out the free video of Grant explaining ZPoint at http://everydaybliss.org/zpointvideo.html.

BASIC BIOENERGETIC THEORY (HOW AND WHY THIS STUFF WORKS)

Childre, Doc, and Howard Martin. 2000. *The HeartMath Solution*, New York, NY: HarperCollins.

Csikszentmihalyi, Mihaly. 1991. *Flow: The Psychology of Optimal Experience*. New York, NY: Harper Perennial.

Diamond, John. 1990. *Life Energy: Using the Meridians to Unlock the Hidden Power of Your Emotions*. St. Paul, MN: Paragon House.

Lipton, Bruce. 2005. *Biology of Belief: Unleashing the Power of Consciousness, Matter, and Miracles*, San Francisco, CA: Mountain of Love Publishing.

McTaggart, Lynne. 2003. *The Field: The Quest for the Secret Force of the Universe*. Whitby, North Yorks, UK: Quill Publishing.

BELIEF SYSTEMS AND THE LAW OF ATTRACTION

Dilts, Robert, Tim Halbom, and Suzi Smith. 1990. *Beliefs: Pathways to Health and Well-being.* Portland, OR: Metamorphous Press.

Dyer, Wayne W. 1995. *Your Sacred Self: Making the Decision to Be Free.* New York, NY: HarperCollins.

————. 1997. *Manifest Your Destiny.* New York, NY: HarperCollins.

————. 2005. *The Power of Intention.* Carlsbad, CA: Hay House.

Hicks, Esther, and Jerry Hicks. 2004. *Ask and It Is Given: Learning to Manifest Your Desires.* Carlsbad, CA: Hay House.

Tolle, Eckhart. 1999. *The Power of Now: A Guide to Spiritual Enlightenment.* Novato, CA: New World Library.

————. 2002. *The Eckhart Tolle Audio Collection (The Power of Now Teaching Series).* Audio CD. Louisville, CO: Sounds True.

————. 2005. *Eckhart Tolle's Findhorn Retreat: Stillness Amidst the World.* Audio CD. Novato, CA: New World Library.

———. 2006. *A New Earth: Reawakening to Your Life's Purpose*. New York, NY: Plume Publishers.

———. 2006. *Practicing Presence: A Guide for the Spiritual Teacher and Health Practitioner*. Audio CD. Vancouver, BC: Eckhart Teachings.

BLISS KEY COMPANIONS

Campbell, Joseph, and David Kudler. 2004. *Pathways to Bliss: Mythology and Personal Transformation*. Novato, CA: New World Library.

Ferris, Timothy. 2007. *The 4-Hour Workweek: Escape 9-5, Live Anywhere, and Join the New Rich*. New York, NY: Crown Publishers.

George, Kimberly. 2006. *Coaching into Greatness: 4 Steps to Success in Business and in Life*. Hoboken, NJ: Wiley.

Louden, Jennifer. 2000. *The Comfort Queen's Guide to Life: Create All That You Need with Just What You've Got*. New York, NY: Harmony Books. **Note:** this book is written with so much love that you'll learn without even realizing it and be able to leverage higher and higher levels of comfort and bliss in your life. Very highly recommended!

———. 2007. *The Life Organizer: A Woman's Guide to a Mindful Year. Tips, Stories, and Prompts to Focus Your Needs and Navigate Your Dreams*. Novato, CA: New World Library.

Lysne, Robin Hereens. 1997. *Sacred Living: A Daily Guide*, Berkeley, CA: Conari Press.

Ryan, M. J. 1999. *Attitudes of Gratitude: How to Give and Receive Joy Every Day of Your Life*. Berkeley, CA: Conari Press.

ENERGY THERAPIES, SYSTEMS, AND TRAINING

Ball, Ron, ed. 2006. *Freedom at Your Fingertips*, Fredericksburg, VA: Inroads Publishing.

Brennan, Barbara Ann. 1993. *Light Emerging: The Journey of Personal Healing.* New York, NY: Bantam.

Childre, Doc, and Howard Martin. 2000. *The HeartMath Solution*, New York, NY: HarperCollins.

Davis, Martha, Matthew McKay, and Elizabeth Robbins Eshelman. 2000. *The Relaxation and Stress Reduction Workbook.* Oakland, CA: New Harbinger Publications.

Eden, Donna. 1999. *Energy Medicine.* New York, NY: Tarcher/Penguin Group. **Note:** If you read no other book, read Donna's. Her meridian system, based on kinesiology and the meridian acupressure of Touch for Health, is presented in an easily accessible format. (If you want to study the origins of this work, see John Thie's *Touch for Health* below.)

Eden, Donna, David Feinstein, and Gary Craig. 2005. *The Promise of Energy Psychology.* New York, NY: Tarcher/Penguin Group.

Gallo, Fred, and Harry Vincenzi. 2000. *Energy Tapping.* Oakland, CA: New Harbinger Publications.

Thie, John. 1973. *Touch for Health: A Practical Guide to Natural Health with Acupressure Touch*. Camarillo, CA: DeVorss & Company. **Note:** the first of the energy therapies, this meridian-based healing system from the 1970s is still the most comprehensive. Very highly recommended.

SUPPORTIVE PRACTICES

Brantley, Jeff, and Wendy Millstine. 2005. *Five Good Minutes: 100 Morning Practices to Help You Stay Calm and Focused All Day Long*. Oakland, CA: New Harbinger Publications.

Cameron, Julia. 1992. *The Artist's Way: A Spiritual Path to Higher Creativity*. New York, NY: Jeremy P. Tarcher.

Chodron, Pema. 2003. *Uncomfortable with Uncertainty: 108 Teachings on Cultivating Fearlessness and Compassion.* Boston, MA: Shambhala Publications Inc.

Hay, Louise L. 1999. *You Can Heal Your Life*. Carlsbad, CA: Hay House.

Tourles, Stephanie. 2001. *How to Feel Fabulous Today: 250 Simple and Natural Ways to Achieve Spiritual, Emotional, and Physical Well-Being*, New York, NY: MJF Books Fine Communications.

Vitale, Joe and Bill Hibbler. 2006. *Meet and Grow Rich: How to Easily Create and Operate Your Own "Mastermind" Group for Health, Wealth, and More*. Hoboken, NJ: Wiley.

Weil, Andrew. 1997. *Eight Weeks to Optimum Health: A Proven Program for Taking Full Advantage of Your Body's Natural Healing Power*. New York, NY: Ballatine Books.

References

Ball, Ron, ed. 2006. *Freedom at Your Fingertips*, Fredericksburg, VA: Inroads Publishing.

Cameron, Julia. 1992. *The Artist's Way: A Spiritual Path to Higher Creativity*. New York, NY: Jeremy P. Tarcher.

Childre, Doc and Howard Martin. 2000. *The HeartMath Solution*. New York, NY: HarperCollins.

Connolly, Grant. 2006. *The ZPoint Process for Instant Emotional Healing*. Revised ed. Toronto, Canada: Self-published. Retrieved from www .zpointprocess.com in May 2007.

Craig, Gary. 2006. *The EFT Manual*. 6th ed. The Sea Ranch, CA: Self-published. Retrieved from www.emofree.com in February 2006.

Csikszentmihalyi, Mihaly. 1991. *Flow: The Psychology of Optimal Experience*. New York, NY: Harper Perennial.

Fleming, Tapas. 1999. *You Can Heal Now*. Redondo Beach, CA: TAT International.

George, Kimberly. 2006. *Coaching into Greatness: 4 Steps to Success in Business and in Life*. Hoboken, NJ: Wiley.

Kiecolt-Glaser, Janice K., Ronald Glaser, and Lynanne McGuire. 2002. Psychoneuroimmunology: Psychological influences on immune function and health. *Journal of Consulting and Clinical Psychology* 70(3):537-547.

Nims, Larry. 1999. *The Original Be Set Free Fast Training Manual*. Orange, CA: Self-published.

Thie, John. 1973. *Touch for Health: A Practical Guide to Natural Health with Acupressure Touch*. Camarillo, CA: DeVorss & Company.

Tolle, Eckhart. 1999. *The Power of Now: A Guide to Spiritual Enlightenment*. Novato, CA: New World Library.

University of Illinois Medical Center at Chicago. 2004. Depression, Stress, and Heart Disease. Retrieved from http://uimc.discovery-hospital.com/main.php?t=symptom&p=heart_disease_stress on February 27, 2007.

Weil, Andrew. 1997. *Eight Weeks to Optimum Health: A Proven Program for Taking Full Advantage of Your Body's Natural Healing Power*. New York, NY: Ballatine Books.

Maryam Webster, M.Ed., enjoyed her career as a transpersonal psychotherapist and practitioner of energy psychology for twenty years, then retrained as a personal performance coach. She merged powerful energy psychology techniques with high-performance coaching methods to create the new field of energy coaching. In addition to directing The Energy Coach® Institute and leading its Certified Energy Coach® Program, Maryam works with women in leadership positions, helping them to regain their bliss to excel both at work and at home.

Maryam is both a current member and a former board member of the Association of Comprehensive Energy Psychology. She is also a contributing member of the International Association of Coaching, the Institute of Noetic Sciences, and the Institute for the Advanced Studies of Health. Maryam continues to develop the field of energy coaching, providing both advanced training and research to the professional community. She lives in the San Francisco Bay Area.

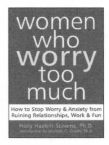